The Pastor's Guide to Fund-Raising Success

Rev. Dr. Dorsey E. Levell and
Wayne E. Groner

Bonus Books, Inc.
Chicago

Copyright © 1999 by Bonus Books, Inc.

Library of Congress Cataloging-in-Publication Data

Groner, Wayne E. –
Levell, Dorsey E.
    The Pastor's Guide to Fund-Raising Success   1st Ed.

ISBN 1–56625–123–0

Bonus Books, Inc.
160 East Illinois Street
Chicago, IL 60611

First Edition

Printed in the United States of America

Contents

Checklist for Success

Celebrate Success

Cecil B. DeMille and Stewardship

Affirming the Stewardship of Environment

Affirming the Stewardship of Money

Affirming the Stewardship of Giftedness

Affirming the Stewardship of Service

A Tale of Two Churches

The White Rabbit

Checklist for Success

Celebrate Success

List of Tables

Acknowledgments

We gratefully acknowledge and thank the following persons, whose help made this a better book than it would have been otherwise:

Carol Dunning, G.B. Dunning, Gene Groner, Carolyn Levell, Kenny Qualls, and Ken Schnell, for their encouragements, their strong foundations of faith, and their insights based on many years of teaching, preaching, and counseling.

Gene Akeman, Jason Alexander, Jody Burzinski, Coleen Carter, Charles Chance, Rosemary Chance, Phylis Coomes, Bob Hartsook, John Joslin, Mary Margaret Mooney, Tony Rabig, Frankie Reynolds, Paula Ringuette, Jeff Tjiputra, and Bob Warford, for their assistance with research and technical matters. Their expertise was invaluable. They were always friendly, always available, and always supportive.

Special thanks to Judith Nichols, whose early encouragement strengthened our commitment to write this book.

Introduction

In a corporate training room employees were asked to make commitments to minor changes in their daily routines for a period of one week. The commitments were written on large sheets of newsprint taped to the wall. Each commitment was signed by an employee. Included were promises to:

"Park my car facing away from the building instead of toward it."

"Put on my make-up before breakfast rather than after."

"Carry my office keys on the left side of my belt instead of the right side."

"Prepare school lunches for my children the night before instead of in the morning."

"Not watch television after 10 P.M."

"Take a different route to work."

Some employees were not able to keep their commitments. Others who kept their commitments said it was a struggle to change firm habits.

Change can cause stress. It can also be transforming for our own good and the good of a greater cause. The lives of twelve men were changed forever when they accepted Jesus' call to be his apostles. The twelve followed him in faith, not always understanding what he was about nor what he expected of them.

Fund raiser and *volunteer* were not terms used in Jesus' ministry, even though the concepts were practiced. Several women used their own financial resources to provide food, clothing, and shelter for Jesus and his apostles. It is not a big leap to consider the women likely enlisted others to do the same. The tomb of Jesus was a major gift. Today, we would call it a gift-in-kind.

In the Old Testament, Job, Isaiah, Micah, and Amos were among those who preached that it is compassionate and just to help the needy. In the New Testament, Jesus said whenever we help the sick, the poor, and the condemned we have ministered to Him. Today, many pastors and other church leaders understand the need for money to fund church ministries. Too many of them do not understand the role of fund raising as an integral part of church activities.

At first, you may find it uncomfortable, even stressful, to apply the proven fund-raising techniques we describe and recommend. Some pastors and other church leaders avoid the discomfort and stress of the topic simply by not talking about it. Or, if the subject comes up, they do not use the words *fund raising*. Instead, they talk generically of *philanthropy* or *support for our ministries*. Fear of alienating members and fear of failure are common among church leaders who do not understand the principles and practices of contemporary fund raising.

For many people, fund raising ranks next to public speaking as the most stressful thing to do. In public speaking, fears are put to rest when the speaker knows the subject, knows the skills, knows the audience, and gets through a few successes. It is the same with fund raising. That is, knowledge enables effective management of the risks. We wrote this book to take the mystery, and thus the fear, out of fund raising for you and your church.

When you know and use the fund-raising process it will be less mysterious and frightening, and more manageable and useful. Corporate executives, real estate developers, investors, politicians, military personnel, and sports professionals are among those who make it their business to recognize risk, assess it, and manage it. No sane person jumps out of an airplane without a parachute. The risk is too great. However, thousands of skydivers jump out of airplanes every day wearing parachutes. It is still a risk, but the risk has been identified and managed at a level that is acceptable to the jumpers. We ask you to consider the principles and practices we have written about to be your parachute.

Our book has two premises. One, the pastor must be personally and actively involved in securing funds for church ministries. The pastor must know who gives how much and be prepared to ask for gifts, especially big gifts. We tell why and show how to do it. Two, securing funds for church ministries must be planned, organized, implemented, and ongoing in conjunction with other church programs. Funding does not happen just because you are doing God's work, and fund raising is not something you do once a year or only when there are crises. We show how to make fund raising an integral part of your church's activities.

All of us are stewards, struggling with our responses to the love of God. His love for us began with our creation and our stewardship began when He put us in charge of all living things. Besides caring for the environment, the Bible identifies money, giftedness, and service to others as major areas of our stewardship. It is beyond the scope of our book to give in-depth coverage to these. We focus on one aspect of financial stewardship: programs which enable and encourage all of us to respond to God's love with our dollars for ministries.

If you are a pastor, our book will help you become a more effective leader, manager, and shepherd. For other church leaders and members, our book will help strengthen your motivation, help you be supportive of your pastor, and open opportunities for the love of God to enter deeper into your lives.

Each chapter begins with a theme-setting dialogue. Chapter One looks at the characteristics of an effective pastor/fund raiser and spells out what is expected of the pastor, governing board, and members when it comes to fund-raising initiatives. Chapter Two explains what motivates people to give, and covers the three types of fund-raising programs — annual giving, capital campaign, and endowment — and when your church should use them. Chapter Three focuses on ways of meeting donors' needs; tells why churches should think programs and ministries first, then dollars; and explains the fund-raising process. Chapter Four tells how to create a 14-month fund-raising plan for your church in the context of stewardship education. Chapter Five details the steps in asking for the major gift, including what to do when you get turned down. Chapter Six covers issues of ethics and accountability, and how gift acceptance guidelines speak effectively to those issues. Chapter Seven briefly explores the major themes of biblical stewardship as they apply to giving and fund raising.

Bible references are suitable for use with all versions.

Each chapter ends with sections called Checklist for Success and Celebrate Success. These are action steps you can take to implement the principles and practices we cover. The sections refer you to other parts of the book and to other resources.

The appendices have definitions of fund-raising terms, a code of ethical practices, a donor's bill of rights, professional development resources, guidelines for selecting a fund-raising consultant, sample contracts for guidance in dealing with consultants, where to find fund-raising helps on the World Wide Web, sample bylaws for a church foundation; suggested readings on related topics we hope you will want to know more about; and a list of directories, periodicals, and subscription services.

Some denominations may have guidelines for their local congregations on fund raising, including specifics on tithing, special projects, and how funds raised may be used. Our book is not meant to circumvent these guidelines. Rather, we hope it will provide insights that will enable you to get started, or to strengthen what you are already doing.

1
Characteristics of an Effective Pastor/Fund Raiser

Now, wait just a minute. With all the things I have to do as pastor, you want me to become a fund raiser, too?"

We know you have a big load with preaching, teaching, visiting in homes, counseling married couples and individuals, and managing budgets, staff, and volunteers. We believe you can integrate sound fund-raising practices into what you are already doing, and look for new ways to help members respond.

"I became a pastor to bring souls to Christ. We're doing God's work and that should be enough to motivate members. I'm not going to beg them for contributions."

Even though the power of God can influence our lives to move forward His important work, He expects us to do many things on our own initiatives. Churches cannot survive and grow on faith alone. It takes money for maintenance and outreach. Effective fund raising strengthens and extends church ministries and gives members more opportunities to honor God by returning their financial blessings to His work.

*"I tried fund raising once and it didn't work. At the end of the year
I wrote a letter to each family and asked them to give an extra $25 per
member so we could meet our budget. Only three families responded,
giving a total of $110. Was that ever embarrassing. Never again for
me."*

Successful fund raising, much like the principles of the
gospel, is a process. The process is to identify, cultivate, and
ask prospective donors for their commitments. When you
integrate the fund-raising process into your church programs it works, just as the principles of the gospel work to
bring persons to Christ. What is the fund-raising plan you
are using now?

*"Plan? I don't have time for planning. I have too many flash fires
to put out. Besides, fund raising is something the women and youth
departments do. They do it pretty well, too, with their bazaars, chili
suppers, and car washes. And, I give my tithing sermon every year just
before Thanksgiving."*

So, you are saying that you have more than enough
money to fund all of your ministries.

"No pastor is prepared to say that."

If we showed you some basic fund-raising techniques
that have worked for churches and other nonprofits all over
the country, enabling you to build upon your faith and your
management skills as a pastor, would you consider trying
some new approaches to fund raising?

"That sounds like a trick question."

What we propose has nothing to do with tricks. It is
based on sound fund-raising principles we have used and
seen work during our more than fifty years of combined service to churches, clients, and employers. Would you consider giving us a fair try?

"Well, yes, since you put it that way, I think I would consider it."

Great, let's get started! We caution you it won't be easy
to change old habits. But, with new insights and new tools
you will be on your way to new fund-raising successes.

The Pastor is Responsible for Fund Raising

If your church has fund-raising efforts that do not produce the results you desire, we challenge you to new successes with programs and planning that go beyond chili suppers, candy sales, and the annual tithing sermon. Churches of all sizes need money for current operations, missions, and capital improvements. As pastor, you are responsible for the fund-raising success of your church by creating and implementing programs to identify, cultivate, and ask members for their financial support. You are responsible for the impact fund raising has on individual and congregational stewardship. It is not a matter of choosing whether to be a stewardship leader. "The pastor can only choose whether to be a *competent* or an *incompetent* stewardship leader," says stewardship specialist Wayne C. Barrett.[1] You should actively engage in fund raising, not just delegate or oversee it.

Many pastors are reluctant and even fearful of actively soliciting funds for one or more of the following real or perceived reasons:

1. They do not understand the techniques of successful fund raising.
2. They think fund raising is begging.
3. They think fund raising programs will turn off members.
4. They tried it and it did not work.
5. They think fund raising is somebody else's job.
6. They think because they are doing's God's work members naturally will be motivated to give.
7. They think an annual tithing sermon is sufficient.

Your Built-in Strengths

Church researcher George Barna declares: "Most pastors, church staff and lay leaders are both inadequately trained and emotionally unprepared for communicating about and actually raising the kind of money required to lead a church toward the fulfillment of its vision."[2] If you recognize these conditions in yourself, we assure you they are not fatal. As pastor, you have several things going for you to overcome fear of fund raising.

One, you understand how to bring persons to Christ, which means you have a foundation for understanding the basic steps to fund-raising success. In bringing persons to Christ you identify your prospects, involve them in church activities, then invite them to receive Christ. That is the pattern of successful fund raising — identify, cultivate, and ask.

Two, you are pastor because of your faith, knowledge, skills, and desires. These are also some of the characteristics of an effective fund raiser, even though Fund Raising 101 was probably not offered in seminary. Most seminaries focus on scholarly and religious studies, preparing students to be preachers and counselors, not leaders and managers. Not only are the principles and practices of fund raising not taught in most seminaries, neither are the principles and practices of stewardship.[3]

Three, the history of giving is on your side. People want to give. They just need a little help. Individuals make up the largest group of contributors, and churches receive the largest portion of individual gifts, though not the majority of gifts.[4] When you create opportunities for giving, members, visitors, and friends are able to find their individual levels of joyful response to the love of God.

Four, you have a captive audience. Hopefully, most of those who come to your church are on a faith journey to the perceived same destination, and they want to get there successfully, even though it is unlikely that all are at the same understanding of faith. Purposeful giving involves them in

God's work, and thus it has the capacity to strengthen their faith, enlarge their worship, and fulfill their stewardship.

We are not suggesting that church giving will guarantee givers a select place in heaven. In doing the Lord's work, we are guided by the ideals of service, reconciliation, and healing. Money is only one part of our personal and corporate stewardship. However, even though faith can move mountains and even though we cannot live by bread alone, most of us must work for income to provide food, clothing, shelter, transportation, and leisure activities. When we contribute our hard-earned money to our church or to charity, we want to see results that validate our values.

The Giving Record

It is true church members should give regularly and sacrificially because it is the right thing to do. As a practical matter we know many do not. Even though total *dollar* amounts of annual giving to religion in the U.S. have been increasing since the 1960s, the *portion* of after-tax income given to religion has been decreasing, confirming that we do not need to go out of our way to prevent giving. Among twenty-nine Protestant denominations, the annual portion of personal after-tax income given to church went from 3.11% in 1968 to 2.46% in 1995. During the same period, per capita income increased by 68%, after taxes and inflation were factored out.[5]

"Had giving to religion increased at a rate commensurate with the changes in income," report church researchers John and Sylvia Ronsvalle, "the total amount of giving to religion in 1995 would have been . . . $99.2 billion" rather than $44.5 billion.[6]

As manager, leader, and shepherd, the pastor is responsible for every aspect of local church life, including fund raising. The pastor must know who gives what and when in order to effectively plan, teach, manage, preach, exhort, counsel, and lead.[7] Giving levels are signs of commitment levels and help the pastor select key leaders. Changes in giving levels may indicate need for a pastoral visit to counsel personal or health problems.[8]

Fund-raising techniques are not a substitute for a committed faith and a willing heart. In and of themselves, techniques will not change your members' attitudes regarding giving. What they will do is create situations in which members can more effectively respond to God's love with their financial gifts in support of church ministries. In other words, fund-raising techniques help your members do the right thing.

"When we give to others, when we share our time, talent, and treasure, we do not end up with less in our accounts, but more," says stewardship consultant Douglas M. Lawson.[9]

What the Pastor Brings to the Table

Many of the characteristics of an effective pastor/fund raiser are the same as those of corporate managers and non-profit executives. A sampling is shown in Table 1.1.

In the first comprehensive, national study of fund raisers — sponsored by the National Society of Fund Raising Executives (NSFRE) and the Lilly Endowment — researchers concluded that the fund raisers surveyed "had high expectations of their fund-raising colleagues, prized traits that indicate strong characters and warm personalities, and acknowledged the importance of skills and knowledge in successful fund raising."[10]

In any business there are the basics. Engineers have to know how to read blueprints. Stock brokers must know which stocks to buy, and when to buy and sell. Carpenters have to know the difference between a level and a power drill. Pastors must know the theology of their faith. In today's world, pastors must also know about fund raising,

Table 1.1 Characteristics of an Effective Pastor/Fund Raiser

Creative and effective manager of personnel and programs

Progressively increasing levels of responsibilities

Strong organizational, communication, and listening skills

Understands the principles and practices of fund raising

Understands the role of fund-raising as a help to members to respond to the blessings of God

Asks for the gift and teaches others to ask

Skilled and experienced at identifying, enlisting, and managing volunteers

Ability to work independently and as a team member

Works well under pressure and multiple deadlines

Initiative and follow-through

Excellent marketing instincts

Computer literate

Sensitive to the needs of diverse constituencies

Results oriented

---

even though fund raising is not a usual clergy attribute. Pastors must be prepared to get the gift, by personally asking for it, by involving others in the process, and by developing fund-raising programs that work. Practice and experience at integrating fund-raising techniques into your church programs will result in confidence and success.

"When we walk to the edge of all the light we have and take that step into the darkness of the unknown," writes poet and pastor Patrick Miles Overton, "we must believe that one of two things will happen. There will either be something solid for us to stand on. Or, we will be taught how to fly."[11]

Chapter Three has more on the fund-raising process and Appendix IX will get you started with some resources for self-study. Besides knowing fund-raising methods through training, practice, and continuing education; having management and organizational skills; and having a commitment to your faith, here are seven essentials of the effective pastor/fund raiser:

1. Be a giver before you become an asker.

Look at your checkbook. Have you been making regular gifts to your church? To community organizations? You cannot be credible in asking others to give if you are not a giver. If you are selling new cars, shouldn't you drive the brand you sell? If you tell others it is important to have a will, shouldn't you have a will? Nothing makes you more credible and strengthens the likelihood of your success as when you can honestly say to a prospective donor: "I have made my personal gift (or pledge) to this program. Won't you join me?" The asker who is a giver has the additional joy of helping another person to enjoy giving. See Table 1.2 on how to create a personal giving plan.

2. Put the interests of the donor first.

The easy thing to say to a prospective donor is, "This is what our church needs." The challenge is to find out the prospect's needs, interests, and potential giving level and to match those with your church's program. Before you ask for the gift, be sure you are wearing your how-may-I-help-you? hat. Is the prospect interested in capital improvements, youth ministries, or missions? Public recognition or anonymity? Giving $100 or $100,000? Making a one-time gift or a multi-year pledge? Giving from current cash or waiting for time-sensitive investments to mature? Other non-profit organizations? Helping the prospect to make a gift commitment that is tailored to the prospect's needs — faith-affirming or otherwise — will save embarrassments, reduce delays, and result in more gifts from happier donors.

Table 1.2 How to Make Your Personal Plan for Giving

Step One
List your charitable interests in priority order. If your list has ten or more entries you probably will be stretching your dollars too thinly. Three to five should be plenty. Include those programs, services and agencies that bring you the most satisfaction. From the standpoint of a giver, your needs are more important than the needs of the charities. Your list could be based on your own devotional experiences and how you feel you have been led by God. Charities you have done volunteer work for are also options.

Step Two
Discuss your plans with family members and your financial advisors for help in turning your plans into actions. Advisors may include your accountant, lawyer, insurance agent, and stock broker.

Step Three
Tithe according to the directives of your faith. Tithing can be to other than your local church. Decide on a regular giving pattern for your tithes, offerings, and other gifts: monthly, quarterly, semi-annually, or annually.

Step Four
Determine how you will contribute your surplus assets during your lifetime and how they will be distributed from your estate. Consult with your family and advisors to explore the options that best fit your needs. Begin with life insurance and a will. Provide for your family first, then your charitable interests. If you do not have family, treat your charitable interests as though they were your children, giving or leaving a portion of your assets to each.

Step Five
Review your plans once each year. Be prepared to make adjustments as your interests and priorities change, including adjustments to your charitable estate plan. Keep in mind it is unlikely you will be able to accomplish in one year everything you want to do with your gift dollars.

3. Be ethical, honest, and open.

Situations will come up that will test your ability to respond appropriately. Keep your standards high. Do not say or do anything that would cause anyone to think badly of you, your church, or your fund-raising program. Among the no-nos are: accepting personal gifts of cash or merchandise from a prospect or donor, reporting oral pledges (all pledges should be written), revealing the dollar amounts of gifts and pledges of others without their permission, promising recognition or benefits you cannot deliver or which you are unauthorized to offer, soliciting for another cause in which you are involved when you call on a prospect for your church program, asking for gifts to programs which have not been approved by your board, accepting a gift with strings attached without approval of your board. See Chapter Six for more on ethics and accountability.

4. Accept defeat without personalizing.

Not everyone will say yes to your request for a gift. No matter how committed you are, no matter how strong your case for support, no matter how easy you make it for the prospect to give, not everyone will say yes. Even top sales professionals get turned down. Keep in mind prospective donors usually are not turning *you* down, they are turning down *your proposal* because it does not meet their needs and interests. Your challenge is to find their needs and interests and to adjust your proposal accordingly. Was the ask amount too high? Are the pledge terms too restrictive? Did the donor think a check must be written at this setting for the full amount? Can the gift be made by a combination of cash, life insurance, or bequest? Is the program something with which the prospect really wants to be involved?

5. Be comfortable with wealthy persons.

Wealthy givers want the same things as non-wealthy givers — appreciation and recognition, assurance their gifts will be spent according to their desires, and confidence the church will be a responsible steward of its assets. Wealthy persons want to see the benefits of their gifts. They want to know that their giving will make a difference. To be comfortable with wealthy people you need to respect them as individuals, know they can understand and appreciate a strong case for support of your fund-raising program, and realize that as members of your church family they have a built-in empathy for your ministries. See Chapter Five for more on attitudes of wealthy persons regarding giving and volunteering.

6. Make face-to-face calls.

There are only four ways to ask for the gift: by mail, by telephone, by pulpit appeals, and face-to-face. The best way, as it is with the gospel appeal, is face-to-face. It enables you to point out the key features of your program that are most appealing to the prospect, share the benefits of the program using your personal enthusiasm, and to respond on the spot to objections the prospect may have. Many face-to-face calls are made by two persons, often the pastor and a volunteer who is a peer of the prospect. Two persons strengthen each other's testimony. Together they can more readily answer objections, and the peer may, for example, say, "I've made my $25,000 gift to our program and I invite you to match it." Did not Jesus send the twelve and the seventy out two by two?

7. Understand the commitment of time and energy.

There is no easy way to be successful. Fund raising is stressful ministry. An unrealistic view of what it takes to do fund raising will make your job even more stressful. As with other aspects of the pastorate, fund raising can affect family life and personal health because of constant pressures to produce desired results. Taking ten names to call on is not as easy as it sounds. So, requiring your board members and volunteers to do so may be setting them up for failure. Building relationships takes time.

What the Church Brings to the Table

There is more to this work than simply being an outstanding pastor/fund raiser. As pastor, you cannot do it alone. Your board and your members have a responsibility to support church fund-raising programs. Boards and members bring their time, talents, and treasures to the table. Their involvement is crucial to success. As they understand and respond as individual donor/stewards, and bring their understandings to bear on the church body, your church will grow in faith, hope, and love, those abiding traits Paul speaks of so eloquently in I Corinthians, Chapter 13. Full funding of church ministries begins to become achievable.

Many highly successful corporations have discovered the benefits of enabling workers to do their jobs more safely, more comfortably, more conveniently, and with more individual decision-making. These corporations provide such things as on-the-job daycare centers, flex-time, skills training, professional development opportunities, and a choice of pay or time off for overtime. The best companies to work for have leadership that inspires self worth, workplaces that are employee friendly, and missions that are customer focused.[12] The results are happier employees who are more productive and make better products or provide better services.

The features of the best companies are also the features church boards and members should support to encourage worship, study, and evangelism. Boards and members sometimes forget — or do not realize in the first place — they must also have in place, or be prepared to create, an environment conducive to successful fund raising. They may think because they are engaged in a wonderful work of high calling that the dollars will come pouring in with little planning and effort. Or, that when fund-raising activities are undertaken, someone in the church — however inexperienced or untrained in fund raising — can be put in charge and be expected to bring in lots of money quickly because that person is so strongly committed to the cause that he or she will succeed without support.

Enthusiasm is a valuable attribute. Enthusiasm without structure and focus can be disastrous — for the fund raiser and for your church. Structure, focus, and a commitment to success are what the board brings to fund-raising, in concert with members' support of budgets and programs. Here are six essentials your board needs to position your church for fund-raising successes:

1. Be givers and askers.

Board members should be making regular contributions to the church and be prepared to ask others to give. Leadership and responsibility start with the board. They must be example setters with their church giving and their commitment to fund-raising programs. The church should be one of the top three non-profits they support. If it is not, they have no business being on the board.

2. Put fund-raising programs in writing.

See Chapters Three and Four for more on program planning. The programs should be written by the pastor and approved by the board, establishing mutual agreement on program directions and expected results. Review the programs at least annually and make any needed adjustments.

3. Have board-approved gift acceptance guidelines.

At minimum, the guidelines should detail the kinds of gifts the church will accept, under what circumstances certain gifts will not be accepted, how gifts will be accounted for and acknowledged, how donors will be recognized, investment policies, whether an annual report will be issued and when and by whom, and a statement that an annual audit will be issued. Review the guidelines at least annually and make adjustments as needed. See Chapter Six on how to write gift acceptance guidelines.

4. Realize it may take a while for fund-raising programs to be successful.

Develop programs with reasonable expectations, but which challenge the pastor, board members, and other church members. While a finger-in-the-dike approach solves the immediate problem, it is no solution for the long term. Planning is the most important asset in establishing fund-raising success.

5. Support the pastor with a meaningful budget for fund raising.

This includes an up-to-date computer and software, a printer, access to the Internet, office space and furniture, and secretarial help — either paid or volunteer. The budget should include funds for the pastor to attend workshops and conferences, subscribe to professional publications, join professional and community service organizations, and for the pastor's out-of-pocket expenses such as meals with prospective donors.

6. Establish a board-development committee.

This committee should be charged with doing for the board what the board requires of the pastor — keeping current on the issues. This includes issues of board management, personnel, fund-raising techniques, the pastorate, and faith curriculum. Board members should attend fund-raising workshops and conferences, subscribe to fund-raising publications, and be actively engaged in community service organizations.

Should Your Church Hire
A Staff Fund Raiser?

Whether your church membership is large or small, the techniques and programs described in this book can be done by pastors, board members, or volunteers. If membership is small — a Sunday morning attendance of less than 100 persons — it is unlikely you need to hire a staff fund raiser.

If your church is large — approaching or exceeding 2,000 persons — your funding needs may be complex and you may wish to consider hiring a staff fund raiser. Large churches have opportunities to spread fund-raising activities among a greater number of talented volunteers operating in several committees, with or without a staff fund raiser. Greater participation strengthens ownership of fund-raising programs and helps assure success in large and in small churches.

You Have Options

Large or small, you have options. Some churches have a financial secretary who handles cash receipts, makes bank deposits, prepares thank-you letters for the pastor's signature, prepares gift-reminder letters, and schedules visitations. After carefully reviewing this person's skills and other qualifications, you may wish to provide fund-raising training for that person. See Appendix IV for some training resources. Clearly-defined fund-raising duties could be added to the financial secretary's job description. The secretary could become a development assistant to the pastor or perhaps the church's full-time staff fund raiser.

Retired fund raisers or persons getting started in consulting are sometimes available and may be willing to work out of their homes. Consultants are prepared to provide services for one or two days each month, manage special events, and do writing and public relations work in connection with fund raising on an annual contract basis. Fees can range from $500 to $2,500 per day plus expenses. Be sure the contract clearly spells out what your church will provide and what the consultant will provide.

If you feel there is insufficient activity to justify hiring a consultant on an on-going basis, you may want to contract with a consultant for a specific project. The project should have a stated beginning and ending, specify what services the consultant will provide, and specify expected results, although results cannot be guaranteed. Capital campaigns usually achieve better results with consultants than when the campaigns are self-directed. Consultants bring proven performance, expertise, earned respect, consistent support, and reduced costs.[13] See Chapter Two for more on the role of consultants. A guide to selecting consultants is in Appendix V. Appendix VI has sample consulting contracts.

Consider Volunteers

Another option is to use experienced volunteers. There may be fund raising, marketing, and public relations experts among your members who would manage fund raising activities as volunteers and at no cost other than out-of-pocket expenses. Their roles should be clearly defined and their activities directed to board-approved goals.

If you decide to hire a full-time staff fund raiser you will want to calculate the added costs to your budget of salary, benefits, secretarial help, office supplies and equipment, printing, telephone, and automobile mileage and other travel. Be aware that it may take months or years for fund-raising activities to be totally successful and that not everyone in your church will be fully supportive of the idea that a paid fund raiser is on staff.

CHECKLIST FOR SUCCESS

Date Completed

_____   List the benefits you would like for yourself and your church from reading this book. Check your progress along the way.

_____   Contact your denomination's headquarters for available resources for stewardship, giving, philanthropy, and fund raising. Visit your local library and bookstore. Refer to the appendices in this book.

_____   Join the nearest chapter of the National Society of Fund Raising Executives (NSFRE). Chapters usually meet for a monthly luncheon to hear a guest speaker and to share ideas on what works in fund raising. There are chapters in all large cities and many mid-size cities. To find the address of the chapter nearest you and the name of the chapter president, write to NSFRE, 1101 King Street, Suite 700,

Alexandria, VA 22314-2976, or telephone 800-666-3863. Their website is http://www.nsfre.org. If there is no chapter near you, consider starting one by contacting fund development officers of other nonprofits. NSFRE has personnel to help you and a free kit of materials on how to organize a chapter.

_____ Involve other church leaders in exploring your ideas for developing a greater emphasis on fund raising. A good place to start is with members of your pastor/church relations committee and your stewardship committee.

_____ Make a comprehensive, personal stewardship plan that brings to you the joy of giving. See Table 1.2. You will be a more credible example when your own giving plan is in place and implemented. Ask a key leader of your board to do the same. Then both of you — or the key leader and another board member he or she recruits — should meet with the other board members individually and encourage them to make personal giving plans. Extend this process to your stewardship committee and other leadership groups.

_____ Pastor, review the make-up of your board, stewardship committee, and other key committees to be sure you have the best representation of donor/stewards. Weaknesses may be dealt with by providing additional training or developing replacement leadership. Your stronger, more committed leaders should be able to help this occur. Business as usual is not a choice if your church wants funding for ministries to grow.

CELEBRATE SUCCESS

List the most valuable ideas you received from this chapter. Set target dates and choose people responsible for implementation, including yourself. List ways to articulate to members and friends of the church the intended or anticipated benefits of the ideas. Create ways to celebrate the successful achievement of the benefits.

NOTES

1   Wayne C. Barrett, *More Money, New Money, Big Money* (Nashville: Discipleship Resources, 1989), 51.

2   George Barna, *How to Increase Giving in Your Church* (Ventura, California: Regal Books, 1997), 13.

3   John Ronsvalle and Sylvia Ronsvalle, *Behind the Stained Glass Windows* (Grand Rapids: Baker Books, 1996), 155-164.

4   Ann E. Kaplan, Editor, *Giving USA 1998* (New York: AAFRC Trust for Philanthropy, 1998), 22, 23, 30, 158, 159.

5   Ronsvalle, *The State of Church Giving through 1995* (Champaign, Illinois: empty, tomb, inc. 1997), 11, 13.

6   Ronsvalle, 49.

7   Ronsvalle, *Behind the Stained Glass Windows*, 133-141.

8   Barrett, 59, 60.

9   Douglas M. Lawson, *Give to Live: How Giving Can Change Your Life* (Poway, California: ALTI Publishing, 1991), 188.

10 Margaret A. Duronio and Eugene R. Tempel, *Fund Raisers: Their Careers, Stories, Concerns, and Accomplishments* (San Francisco: Jossey-Bass Publishers, 1997), 159.

11 Patrick Miles Overton, "Faith," *The Leaning Tree* (St. Louis: The Bethany Press, 1975), 91.
12 Ronald B. Lieber, "Why Employees Love These Companies," *Fortune* Jan. 12, 1998: 72-74.
13 Quentin Wagenfield, "Go Pro on Fundraising," *Your Church* May/June 1998: 56+.

2
The Three Types of Fund-Raising Programs and When to Use Them

I can tell you that just declaring our budget needs and expecting members to respond hasn't worked very well to bring in the money. Why is that?"

Individual needs vary dramatically. The budget is only a management tool to help get the job done. And, it is only one tool of several you should use to encourage members to give.

"What are some of the other tools?"

There are three types of fund-raising programs which address the needs of members and the needs of funding ministries: the annual fund, the capital campaign, and the endowment fund. The effective pastor/fund raiser uses all three.

"How will using all of them help?"

They provide the means for reaching members at their many different levels of understandings, interests, and capabilities in two ways: they help members focus on programs and ministries rather than budgets, and they encourage people to give proportionately according to their resources by opening new ways of giving.

"So, the spiritual well-being of members is directly tied to their needs?"

Yes, and your fund-raising programs should reflect that by being more than just weekly offerings or crises appeals. There needs to be variety in fund raising just as in worship, business, and recreation.

"How do I do that?"

Let's start by looking at why people give.

What Motivates People to Give?

The IRS lists more than one million tax-exempt organizations. Approximately one-half are eligible to receive tax-deductible contributions. Another 341,000 religious congregations also are eligible to receive tax-deductible gifts.[1] That is a lot of competition for our gift dollars. Appeals seem to bombard us by television, radio, newspapers, magazines, telephone, direct mail, and pitches at our front door. On top of that, local churches are finding it increasingly difficult to reach a balance between the funding requests of their state and national headquarters and their local operations.

Not everyone gives just because the church or other worthy cause has needs. All good causes are worthy and have needs. People give because giving fulfills *a need in them.* Jesus Christ fulfilled the needs of sinners with the gift of salvation, setting out a step-by-step program for people to accept salvation through faith, repentance, and baptism. These are the principles of the gospel referred to in Hebrews 6:1 and 2.

Roy W. Menninger, president of The Menninger Foundation, says there are three levels of motivation in giving: narcissism, guilt, and selflessness, with selflessness being the most mature level. He cautions that giving is never pure. "The most altruistic and most noble giving also contains elements of narcissism and guilt, and even gifts which seem blatantly self-aggrandizing include an altruistic

Table 2.1 Why People Give to Church[3]

Shared Cause

More than nine out of ten adults who give money to churches say they do so because they are convinced the church believes in and stands for the same things as the donor. This notion of having a shared cause is virtually indispensable in attracting donations.

Ministry Efficiency

Four out of five church donors say they will give only if they are persuaded the church uses people's money carefully and wisely.

Ministry Influence

Four out of five church supporters actively search for evidence that their money has made a difference in people's lives. Most churches struggle to trigger this motivation.

Urgent Need

Six out of ten church donors admit they are more likely to give when they become aware of an urgent need, whether that need emanates from their church or from some other organization.

Personal Benefit

Many people give to their church because they wish to express their gratitude for what the church has done in their own lives or in the lives of people close to them. Frequent but less common motivations for giving included hoped-for benefits to the donor or the donor's loved ones and interests.

Relationship With the Ministry

Six out of ten adults say they give to their church out of a feeling of responsibility or moral obligation to the Christian community to which they

> belong and to the ministries in which
> they participate.

element. . . . Donors and recipients need to feel that the decision to give is justified, and that the transaction concludes with a worthwhile psychological contract."[2]

Mutual benefit is among the reasons for church giving as shown in Table 2.1. Other often-listed reasons include: acceptance, affiliation, fear, guilt, love, memoria, power, pride in achievement, recognition, spiritual need, status, and team success. Tax relief, by itself, seldom motivates giving.

There are several conclusions we can draw from such a list:

People give to meet their needs, not just the needs of the institution.

The challenge is to convince members the church is speaking to their needs, so they will be willing to direct more of their contributions to the local church. We must get over the idea that there is not enough money in our local churches to fund programs and ministries. We do that by developing activities to enable members to give.

*People give when they understand the vision
and mission of the church.*

Church members want, need, and demand that the solution of problems in the local church and the local community be given first priority. Every level of the church leadership needs to connect with the person in the pew. Lack of communication is an almost fatal error of churches which strongly emphasize meeting the budget every year rather than meeting members' needs.

Churches must communicate their vision to members and ask members to support the vision with their gifts. "You have not because you ask not." (James 4:2) Members who see their gifts working toward the church's *vision* (where the church desires to be), and who are recognized and appreciated for their gifts, become meaningful participants in the church's *mission* (activities which achieve the vision). They realize the joy of giving and will give again.

For more on what motivates giving, see Chapter Three.

People give to support programs not budgets.

Most people are not interested in budgets and cannot remember the figures for even a few minutes. They give to see the results of their gifts doing something for someone, including themselves. They expect actions to meet needs and will give where they perceive the action to be. In growing and effective churches — churches which are meeting the needs of members — budgets follow programs.

Per capita giving is often used as a measurement of church support. It is found by dividing the amount of annual contributions by the total number of members. The issue for your church should not be per capita giving alone, which is just one way of measuring effective giving. The issue should be whether there are sufficient contributions, annually and otherwise, to achieve the vision and mission your members have embraced.

The Annual Fund

You should use the annual fund to cover current operations of the church — local, state, and national. Gifts to the annual fund are usually small and from members' current assets. They are often made weekly or monthly. They come from regular offerings, special offerings, targeted gifts, direct mail, special events, and pulpit appeals. Many churches raise their annual funds through some form of every-member campaign, usually by pledge to be fulfilled before the end of the calendar year. Some denominations publish step-by-step annual fund guidelines designed for their local churches. Some churches use non-denominational guidelines available at bookstores.

Not all churches implement a full plan of asking every member to give every year. Some church leaders take short-cuts, thinking: "Our annual fund campaign this year was very successful and it was a lot of hard work. Now that our members know what is expected of them, they will continue to give every year without being asked. After all, we are engaged in the Lord's work and our members know it takes money to get the job done." The result is that annual giving begins to decline. After three or four or five years church leaders decide they had better do another annual campaign.

Such interruptions not only weaken ministries and individual response opportunities, they add to the challenges of helping persons understand the importance of ongoing and increased giving to the church, in good times and in bad times.

Weekly Offerings

Weekly offerings provide opportunities for people to give at their many different financial levels and levels of understanding. Weekly offerings should enable and encourage regular giving. Too often, though, the offertory part of a worship service is perfunctory and non-worshipful, even to the point of subtly discouraging some people from giving.

"Your presentation requires prayerful consideration and serious thought if you are to successfully lead people into the presence of their creator through the commitment of a part of themselves to God," write stewardship leaders Len Young and Ken Schnell. "It should be designed to motivate and challenge the congregation to give in the spirit of love even as

Table 2.2 Do's and Don'ts for the Offertory[5]

Do

1. Provide a sound spiritual base for giving.

2. Keep the membership informed of the financial needs. (This may be done with regular pulpit announcements or bulletin inserts.)

3. Encourage giving according to ability or "proportionate giving."

4. Avoid breaking down the budget and asking each family to give the same amount.

5. Invite people to give.

6. Invite people to put God first in their giving — Firstfruits.

7. Give prayerful consideration to your offertory.

8. Set an example by making your offering.

Don't

1. Beg, scold, or plead for money.

2. Appeal to a "sense of duty" to give, as it can drive people away.

3. Refer to the offering as a "collection."

4. Apologize to the congregation for not being prepared.

God has so abundantly given love to each of us."[4] Their do's and don'ts regarding the offertory:

Here are some ways the congregation may participate more fully in offertory worship:

- Several days before the service, ask one or two persons to prepare testimonies of blessings and successes to be given at the offertory.

- Engage people in conversation at the pulpit regarding their testimonies, again with prior knowledge and adequate time for preparation.

- Use special music by the choir, a soloist, or an ensemble, before or after the offertory, not just during it.

- Ask the congregation to stand and ask members to give a brief testimony to a person next to them.

- Invite the congregation to come to the front and place their offerings into a decorated container, such as a basket with a colorful cloth placed in the bottom and over the sides.

- Distribute a pencil and three-by-five file card to everyone and ask them to write a one-sentence statement of stewardship commitment. The statement does not have to be financial. Ask all to come to the front and place their gifts and cards into the container.

- Have more than one person pray over the offering. Use people of different ages, from children to senior citizens. Prayers from these different perspectives bring richness and completeness to the offertory worship.

- Select people to stand at their pews and read short scriptures, poems, or other material related to the offertory. If your service is in a large sanctuary you may need to provide microphones.

Weekly offerings alone may get some of the bills paid, but they leave no margins for creating and sustaining longer-term programs of ministry. Dependence on weekly offerings can result in crises that focus on meeting the budget rather than vision and mission.

Special Appeals

Special appeals are an excellent way to support budgeted ministries and additional ministry opportunities that come up throughout the year. They should be planned as part of your programs and scheduled on the calendar. Gifts from special appeals can send children to camp, fund a mission trip, buy personal items for nursing home residents or shut-ins, support housing and meals for the poor, provide college scholarships, or do just about anything your members desire. Special appeals are opportunities to suggest memorials and tributes. Special appeals communicate directly to the needs of members, who can respond: "I want to do that."

You can use creative ways for members to respond to special appeals. That is what one church did when it discovered there were rotting gutters and soffits in a relatively new building, the result of a design flaw. One beautiful Sunday morning while the congregation was singing the pastor led them outside to view the damage and then back into the sanctuary, still singing. The pastor asked for a special offering and the next Sunday he announced that more than enough had been contributed. The names of the givers were listed in the church bulletin without the amounts each gave. The pastor did all the right things: he demonstrated the need for support, asked appropriately, and recognized and thanked quickly. The givers came away feeling, "I'm glad I did that."

Another pastor was similarly creative. His church needed a van to transport youth and to pick up non-driving senior citizens. The pastor found a good used van and parked it in front of the church and told the story. Gifts came in so quickly that one elderly lady was upset because she did not have time to contribute before the van was purchased. The pastor assured her she could give a tank of gas periodically as her share in "our bus."

A variation on special appeals are targeted gifts. Targeted gifts are usually asked of a handful of individuals in private rather than of the entire membership from the pulpit or by mail. In the examples of the damaged building and of the van, the pastors could have asked several persons or families for funding. They chose to invite all of the members to help.

Offering Envelopes

If your church has pew racks for offering envelopes be sure someone is assigned to keep the racks filled with envelopes and pencils. Include reply envelopes so members can take them home and return them when they have a need to give. In the upper-right corner of the reply envelope print the following words inside a small box: "Thank you for your extra gift of postage."

If you provide dated offering envelopes, mail them to families monthly rather than yearly or rather than having families pick them up at the church. Mail only the next month's supply during the last week of the month. Include a receipt and thank-you letter from the pastor for their last gift, and a reply envelope. The pastor's letter may be used to explain special financial needs, to ask for gifts, and to report on successful ministries. This gives you twelve opportunities to show appreciation to contributors and to keep families updated on church activities and finances. This is especially helpful for families who may not attend regularly. Include a reply envelope with every thank-you letter and you will be pleased at the number of gifts you receive by return mail.

Mailings

Every mailing that goes out from the church should have a giving opportunity. Listing such opportunities enables members to meet their needs to give. List three to five items that vary in cost. At Christmas time you may want to list a dozen or more items. Mention memorials and tributes. Always include a reply envelope.

You can easily mark your reply envelopes to track mail appeals by holding a stack of the envelopes in one hand and marking the edges with a felt-tipped pen. Different colors of ink represent different types of appeals or dates. Only the office staff will ever see it. This is an inexpensive and easy way to track your bounce-back envelopes. Many times you will find envelopes coming back for different purposes than they were sent, even months later. These persons saved the envelopes to give to meet their needs.

Another use of mail is mailing directly to your entire membership for a specific gift appeal. Small churches can do this with volunteers. Large churches should consider engaging a company which specializes in direct mail services.

Special Events

Special events are an important part of many church's social and financial programs. Chili suppers, car washes, pie making, basketball games, bazaars, and even trips to the Holy Land can be fund raisers. These activities are highly social and meet members' needs to be together for a common cause. Special events are best done by church departments or age groups with the funds raised earmarked for activities in those departments or by those groups. The funds also could be directed toward a needful church project. See Appendix IX for some resources on producing special events for fund raising. As with weekly offerings or any other method of fund raising, do not depend on special events to secure all of the money needed for your annual operations.

Challenge Gifts

Another tool in the annual fund method is the challenge gift. If your church needs $10,000, ask a member or family to give the last $5,000. The challenge is best if it is a named leadership gift, but it can be anonymous. Challenge gifts are an excellent way to raise a lot of money quickly. There is a caveat. Challenge gifts give a big boost to your projects, but they tend to be one-time boosts and often cannot be repeated in following years, even with a different challenge giver. The most effective plan for your annual fund is to secure sustainable gifts year after year.

The Capital Campaign

You should use the capital campaign for constructing buildings or making major renovations. Large gifts for capital purposes are most likely to come from members' invested assets rather than current assets. Many capital gifts, large and small, are in the form of pledges paid over a period of time, such as two to five years. As a general rule, your church can raise three to five times its annual operating budget in a capital campaign without eroding your annual fund. Gifts to the capital campaign are in addition to annual gifts and tithes which sustain your operating budget.

The smaller and more sacrificial gifts to a capital campaign often come from members who make weekly or monthly contributions to the campaign. Many increase their giving to meet the need for a new building and will sustain the increased level for years to come. Thus, a capital campaign can increase the per capita giving of your church. Although back-to-back capital campaigns are the norm in higher education and some other nonprofits with national constituencies, they are often ineffective with local churches because the pool of prospects is limited.

The Feasibility Study

After you have determined that a new building or addition is needed, and you are convinced the construction clearly meets the vision and mission of your church, you should conduct a feasibility study. It is not enough to say, "We need this construction and we can do it." Or, "We don't know where the money will come from, but we will trust the Lord." The Lord had something to say about that.

Table 2.3 Tips on Conducting A Feasibility Self-Study[6]

1. Evaluate church membership and giving records to determine the readiness of your congregation.

2. Communicate to members clearly and succinctly why this project is important now.

3. Enlist the right leaders.

4. Involve the congregation.

5. Allow adequate time.

6. Stress the spiritual.

7. Follow up on pledges.

"If you're planning to build a tower, shouldn't you first determine the cost and whether you have enough money to finish it?" (Luke 14:28)

You may conduct a self-study or hire fund-raising counsel. Tips on a self-study are shown in Table 2.3.

Competent counsel will bring to your campaign a plan and sound advice based on successful performance, and will be up front with you on whether there is enough support to achieve your goal, whether you should scale back your plans, or whether you should not proceed at this time. See Appendix V for a guide to selecting counsel and Appendix VI for sample contracts.

Feasibility studies usually have two basic components: a questionnaire and face-to-face interviews of members by the consultant. In small churches the interviews are with most of the adult members. In large churches the consultant interviews only key volunteer leaders and prospective major donors. The consultant will test a dollar amount to be raised, identify prospective leadership gifts, uncover attitudes of members, and reveal who are likely candidates to chair the campaign and committees.

Do not fall into the trap of letting volunteers give only their time during a campaign. Everyone is a prospective donor. It is a time-tested truth that volunteers give and givers volunteer. This is especially true for board members and other church leaders. When they endorse the idea of a capital campaign they effectively commit themselves to be volunteers and financial contributors.

The Study Questionnaire

A feasibility study questionnaire and a cover letter are mailed to every member or family. They are sent to active and inactive members, including local members and members who have moved away but maintain a relationship with your church and to non-member attendees. The questionnaire usually has no more than ten questions similar to those in Table 2.4. Your consultant will work with you on the precise questions for your situation. A postage-paid reply envelope addressed to the consultant is included in the mailing. The cover letter is on the consultant's stationary and is signed by the consultant. The consultant usually mails the materials.

Approximately three weeks after the survey has been mailed the consultant meets with members individually to review the questions and responses. Members are much more likely to tell the consultant things they would not tell the pastor or board. Perceptions are as much a part of the study as reality, especially when it comes to church leadership. If the leaders do not have the confidence of members the campaign will not succeed. In some situations leaders have agreed to step aside in order to enable the church to grow.

A Discovery Weekend

An effective use of the two basic components of a feasibility study is embodied in what we call a Discovery Weekend. The weekend begins with interviews on a Friday

Table 2.4 Feasibility Study Letter and Questionnaire

May 20, 1998

Dear Mr. and Mrs. Douglas:

Faith Baptist Church is seriously considering launching into a new and exciting adventure of building a Family Life Center. I'm sure you are aware that there are several points of view concerning how or whether we should proceed.

The church board has engaged my firm to determine whether there is sufficient support for a Family Life Center to be built at this time. We ask that you complete the enclosed short questionnaire and return it to me in the envelope provided before June 10.

Your thoughts are very important and will be taken seriously and confidentially.

Thank you.

Sincerely,

Fred A. Hampton
President
Hampton and Associates Consulting

Enclosures

1. Do you feel that Faith Baptist Church should build a Family Life Center? _____

2. Do you feel that the proposed building cost of $1 million to $1.3 million is within the ability of the congregation over a three to five year period? _____

3. If we are to proceed with a Family Life Center what features must be included in the Center to assure the success of the project? Please be specific, such as: kitchen, basketball courts, Sunday School classrooms, and so forth.

   _____

   _____

4. If we are to be successful in raising funds to build the Center who are the key individuals who must be involved in the campaign committee?_____

_____

_____

5. Who in the congregation has the ability to cause the project to succeed? _____

_____

6. In your opinion, who in the congregation has the ability to give a leadership gift of $100,000 to $150,000 over three to five years? _____

_____

7. Does the congregation have confidence in the senior pastoral leadership to see the project through? _____

8. If you are against the project now, what would it take to enlist your enthusiastic support? _____

_____

9. If we proceed with the project where do you see your financial contributions over three to five years?
____ $100,000 or more _____ $50,000 or more
_____ $25,000 or more _____ $10,000 or more
_____ $5,000 or more _____ $1,000 or more
_____ Under $1,000

10. Is there anything on your heart or mind that you want to share confidentially?_____

_____

_____

---

morning. The church secretary or pastor sets up several appointments for the consultant with local leading citizens who do not attend the church, such as a bank president, the superintendent of schools, and a prominent business owner. The consultant interviews these citizens regarding the church, its leadership, and its role in the community.

Friday afternoon and evening and all day Saturday, appointments are scheduled at the church for members to meet with the consultant. Sunday morning, the pastor, or sometimes the consultant, presents a homily on the state of the church. After worship there is a basket dinner or catered meal to hear the report of the consultant. At this point the consultant's report usually is ready only in oral form. The consultant puts it in writing later and sends it to the church board and pastor. Sometimes the consultant appears before the board to give a detailed presentation. It is possible the consultant will recommend not going forward with a campaign, or setting a goal lower or higher than the amount tested.

Some feasibility studies can cover periods of three to six months. In these cases interviews are often done at the workplaces of members. The extent and contents of a study are usually determined by the size of the campaign goal and the number of key prospective donors. Larger goals and more prospects may require more extensive studies, but studies are seldom more complex than what we have outlined.

The Campaign Plan

If the campaign is a "go" and you engage a consultant, the consultant will prepare a detailed campaign plan for your approval that includes: a budget, timelines, training sessions for volunteers, methods for contacting all members for their gifts, suggested printed materials, accounting procedures, methods for recognizing donors, and a victory celebration party. The consultant also recommends cultivation and asking strategies — including who will ask major donors for what amounts — and trains campaign workers. The pastor, board, and volunteers work the plan.

Although you do not have to heed your consultant's advice, it is best to pay close attention. An example of not listening that turned into a costly mistake comes from a church that planned to raise one million dollars to relocate at the edge of the county seat. The campaign consultant advised church leaders not to ask for gifts until he determined their readiness. One member was so excited about the campaign he could not wait to ask an elderly lady who lived in a modest two-bedroom house across the street from the church. When he met with her, she asked a typical question, "What do you think I should give?" He replied, "I think you should give $10,000." She wrote him a check in that amount and the man was elated. Within the next year the woman gave a local university $600,000 because that is the amount the university asked of her.

A capital campaign also can be tied to another goal, as in the case of a church seeking to raise $500,000 to buy a pipe organ. During the feasibility study the consultant received clear signals from members that one million dollars could be raised, with one-half going to an endowment fund for missions. All of the money was raised. The church got a beautiful organ and $30,000 annual income in perpetuity for mission support.

The Endowment Fund

You should use the endowment fund for designated programs such as building maintenance, scholarships and grants, and community outreach. The endowment fund is a pool of invested money from which only the earnings or a portion of the earnings are spent. Gifts to endowment funds often come from bequests, life insurance, trusts, and annuities. Such gifts are referred to as planned gifts. Cash gifts can be made to an endowment fund at any time.

Gifts in memory of loved ones or in honor of esteemed persons are often made to an endowment fund. One woman pledged sacrificially to her church for many years in support of the church's annual operating needs. At her death, a resourceful daughter gave to the church's endowment fund enough to pay her mother's annual pledge forever.

In preparing members to consider planned gifts and gifts to an endowment fund, advise them first to be sure all of their living needs are provided for, as well as any financial needs they may have to provide for family. Also advise them to consult with their attorney and family members before making such gifts.

Administration Plan

Administration of endowment funds can be done through your present church organizational structure. Some local churches prefer to have a separate corporation for administering endowment funds. See Appendix VIII for sample foundation bylaws. Most national denominations have their own endowment funds and guidelines for their local churches. Some denominations provide administrative and investment services for local church endowments, often in the form of regional consortiums. Check with your national headquarters.

Every church needs a plan to receive, administer, and expend endowment funds. Without a plan great controversies can develop when the church accepts a large, unexpected gift, either during the donor's lifetime or from an estate, especially if the donor did not specify a use for the gift. After the excitement of the gift announcement dies down it seems as though every member has his or her own plan for spending the money. Controversies can last for years, disrupting lives, clouding the church's vision, and impeding ministries.

Your church should have a board-approved plan for an endowment fund. A committee of members, including representation from the board, should draft the plan with help from an attorney and a financial advisor. The plan should include a statement of the fund's purpose, what kinds of gifts will be accepted, investment management guidelines, accountability processes including annual audits, and guidelines for distributing income. Income may be distributed for anything that is in harmony with your church's vision and mission, including the broad areas of capital improvements, leadership training, support of social service organizations, development grants to help people help themselves, educational ministries, and evangelism. A payout policy should include a schedule of distributions, such as quartely or semi-annually.

It is also a good idea to specify for what distributions shall not be used. This assures members their contributions are still welcomed and needed for annual operations and other ministries not included in the endowment fund.

An endowment committee, including representation from the board, should be established to administer the endowment fund, including receiving and acting on funding requests from church departments.

Keep Members Fully Informed

All members should be made fully aware of the plan for endowment funds. Members should know how the funds will help the church grow, how endowment gifts are a response to God's love, and how individual donor/stewards will benefit from effective financial planning. Members should receive an annual report of the endowment contributions, earnings, and distributions, including management fees, if any.

Ways to keep members informed include small-group meetings, a stewardship emphasis day, planned giving seminars at the church once or twice a year, direct mail, and placing brief, friendly reminders in the Sunday bulletins, similar to those in Table 2.5.

Some awareness activities might have helped in the following situation. A pastor and his wife served small-town churches until his death at age 65. They had saved $200,000, including a small estate from his father. The widow received a denominational pension and social security income, enough for her needs. She did not have to draw

Table 2.5 Planned Giving One-Liners[7]

1. Preparing an estate plan is good Christian stewardship — saying thanks to God, expressing your love and concern for family, and showing charity toward others.

2. Remember, if you have no will or trust, state laws will determine who will inherit your property at your death. State laws do not include your church or any other charity as a beneficiary.

3. Consider naming the church as a beneficiary in your will or living trust. The gift could be a set dollar amount, a percentage of your estate, the remainder after other gifts are made, or part of the estate left if designated heirs are deceased.

4. Did you know that there is no limit on the size of a charitable gift to the church at the time of your death? No matter how large, the gift is deductible for federal estate tax purposes.

5. Think about the part you want to play in our church's future. You have the opportunity to support this ministry in many ways. Naming the church as a beneficiary in your estate plan, or making an endowment gift, can assure your continued participation in this ministry far into the future.

6. Giving to the church through your will or trust is the most common way to continue your support beyond your lifetime. When your estate plan is prepared, consider a gift to the church.

7. Life insurance is a way to make a larger gift to the church than you might otherwise be able to afford. Consider naming the church as a beneficiary of an insurance policy.

8. Our trustees and pastor enthusiastically support planned giving to our church. Contact them for more information.

9. We accept endowment gifts. The income will be used for special church projects. The principle of the gift is never spent and continues indefinitely.

10. Anyone can give an endowment gift. Any size gift may be made as an endowment. You may do this now or as part of your estate plan.

---

from her invested assets, which were kept in a trust that doubled in value every seven years. When she died at age 86 her estate was worth more than $1.6 million, but she did not leave anything to her church! The church had not shared information with her regarding the benefits of remembering the church in her estate plans. We can only imagine how she and the church would have been blessed had she received some reminders over the years.

CHECKLIST FOR SUCCESS

Date Completed

_____   Pastor, review the giving records of your members, especially large donors and potentially large donors, to determine what they have given and to learn what programs and ministries they prefer to support. This information will enable you to build stronger funding relationships.

_____   Conduct a vision-and-mission exercise with your members. Check with your denomination for recommended materials or your local bookstore or library for non-denominational materials. This type of exercise involves all members and helps determine members' and community needs, identifies the talents of members, and reveals their willingness to volunteer. The exercise should be done every three to five years because memberships and attitudes change. The results of the exercise will give your church a clear picture of desired program ministries.

_____ Review board minutes for any decisions regarding endowment policies and plans and determine whether the policies and plans need updating. If your church does not have an endowment plan, discuss with your board the possibilities and practicalities of developing a plan. See Appendix VIII for sample foundation bylaws.

_____ Review your offering techniques to be sure you are encouraging worship and thanksgiving. Create opportunities to regularly thank the people whose gifts make programs and ministries possible. Involve people of all ages in the offertory. See Appendix IX for some offertory resources.

_____ Make a list of your capital needs and wants. This should include items you wish for and would secure if additional money were available. Do not be concerned with cost. Just write. Make the list as long as you want. Ask all members for their suggestions. After the list has been made, name a committee to prioritize the items needed during the next year, the next three to five years, and the next five to ten years. Now, estimate the cost of each item, and you have the beginnings of a capital development program based on planning and member ownership, not on crises management and leader preferences.

CELEBRATE SUCCESS

List the most valuable ideas you received from this chapter. Set target dates and name persons responsible for implementation, including yourself. List ways to articulate to members and friends of the church the intended or anticipated benefits of the ideas. Create ways to celebrate the successful achievement of the benefits.

NOTES

1   *Trust, Service, and the Common Purpose: Philanthropy and the Nonprofit Sector in a Changing America* (Indianapolis: Indiana University Center on Philanthropy; New York: The American Assembly, 1998), 5.

2   Roy W. Menninger, *The Psychology of Giving* (Topeka: The Menninger Foundation), 2-4. Leaflet article adapted from a speech given at the annual conference of the Council of Foundations, Philadelphia, May 1981.

3   George Barna, *How to Increase Giving in Your Church* (Ventura, California: Regal Books, 1997), 59-66.

4   Len Young and Ken Schnell, *Stewardship Ministries: A Stewardship Resource for Congregational Leaders Supporting Your Community of Joy* (Independence, Missouri.: Reorganized Church of Jesus Christ of Latter Day Saints, 1996), 74.

5   Young and Schnell, 74, 75. Used by permission.

6   Quentin Wagenfield, "Go Pro on Fundraising," *Your Church*, May/June 1998: 56+. Used by permission.

7   Renard Kolasa in *The Abingdon Guide to Funding Ministry, Vol. 1*, Donald W. Joiner and Norma Wimberly, Editors, (Nashville: Abingdon Press, 1995), 117. Used by permission.

3
Meeting the Needs of Donors

I think what you've described so far is the chicken-and-the-egg dilemma. If we had programs that met the needs of members they would give more. But, we can't start or sustain programs without their money."

We wish it were not so, but money is required to implement most ministries. You cannot get programs going without first having funds to support them, even if the funds are out-of-pocket expenses of volunteers. That is why planning is essential. Members desire — even require — a vision and mission they can support. Planning and giving help members become owners of the vision and mission. And, members are your most likely donors.

"Are you saying that in the process of uncovering the needs of members we will discover the programs they are willing to underwrite?"

Absolutely. Most members do not like surprises. They respond best when they see plans and programs that work. When you effectively communicate program benefits that meet the needs of your members, money will follow.

"Which is why budgets must follow programs, right?"

Right. For the most part, members are not interested in the needs of the church, unless the church's needs impact them directly. They certainly are not much interested in balancing the budget, although some declare being interested in fiscal soundness. As a practical matter, members are more interested in programs and ministries that match their personal desires and sense of fulfillment.

"Well, then, show me how planning for donor needs works."

Planning to be Successful

"Okay, let's go."

Those simple words by Dwight Eisenhower to his generals and admirals on the evening of June 5, 1944, launched the invasion of occupied France in what many people consider to be the greatest organizational plan in the history of the world. The next morning Allied troops crossed the English Channel and stormed the beaches of Normandy. Within three weeks the Allies had landed more than one million troops, 566,000 tons of supplies, and 171,000 vehicles. Eleven months later the Germans surrendered, ending the war in Europe.

The plan was conceived by Eisenhower two years earlier when he was chief of the War Department's Operations Division in Washington. After the invasion, Winston Churchill declared, "What a plan!" Joseph Stalin said, "The history of warfare knows no other like undertaking from the point of view of its scale, its vast conception and its masterly execution."[1]

There have been other big plans successfully executed. Among them: the Great Wall of China, the pyramids of Egypt, Hoover Dam, the tunnel under the English Channel, sending men to the moon and bringing them back safely, and the more than 42,000 miles of U.S. interstate highways.[2] We must include God's plans, although they are not fully known to us. The Bible remains the number one selling book of all time throughout the world. Three of the world's great religions — Christianity, Judaism, and Islam — trace their beginnings to Abraham, the father of nations.

The common thread among these and many other plans, big and small, is that they were and are responses to the needs of people. Without a plan the church is destined to an environment of fragmentation and failure in which members are unable to realize their full potential of a meaningful relationship with God. God wants to help us and we must pray for His guidance. We must also take the initiative to develop a plan to facilitate His guidance. (Philippians 3:12-14)

Think Programs and Ministries First

Too many churches approach giving based on what is needed to meet the budget, often losing sight of the needs of members and other donor/stewards. Most persons do not care about the budget as an independent document. Instead, they are interested in programs and ministries that meet their needs. Their needs may be related to the public image of the church, staff and management practices, the physical appearances of church buildings and grounds, parking, and even "their" pew. Needs may also be related to Sunday School classes, youth, the frail elderly, music, family and personal counseling, recognition, salvation, community outreach, and involvement with social service organizations and other nonprofit groups. How well your church meets these and other needs will influence financial giving and volunteer giving.

Count the Ways

Fund-raising consultant Robert F. Hartsook has developed 77 reasons why people respond positively to requests for money. As you look over the list, write down the programs and ministries in your church that match each reason. All of the reasons relate to the needs of donors, even those which are personal or corporate, as in numbers 20, 51, 61, 70 and 77.

1. You ask them to give.
2. They know their gift will make a difference.
3. They know their gift will have an impact.
4. You recognize them for their gifts.
5. You allow them to gain personal connections with other individuals who are passionately involved in some meaningful dimension of life.
6. You allow them to get back at the corrupt or the unjust.
7. They have the discretionary wealth to give it away.
8. They feel it's their duty.
9. You allow them to relieve guilt about ethical, political, or personal transgression, whether real or imagined.
10. You enable them to "do something" about a major problem or issue.
11. You enable them to offer opinions and share their attitudes.
12. You help them to learn about a complex and interesting problem or issue.
13. They are afraid the project will fail without them.
14. You give them the chance to release emotional tension caused by a life-threatening situation, critical emergency, or ethical dilemma.
15. They believe it is a blessing to do so.
16. You give them tax benefits.
17. You give them a chance to be associated with a famous or worthy person.
18. You give them the opportunity to belong to something as a member, friend, or supporter.
19. You give them something tangible in return.
20. They have a philanthropic and giving habit.

21. You help them preserve their world view by validating cherished values and beliefs.
22. They have demonstrated that they support organizations like yours.
23. They know their gifts will accomplish something right now.
24. You appreciate them for their gifts.
25. You acknowledge the values they express in their giving.
26. You encourage them to change people's lives with their gifts.
27. You highlight their worthiness.
28. Others they respect have given and invited them to make a gift.
29. You aid them in doing something for a family member, friend, child, or grandchild.
30. You show them a way to make a gift and get a personal return.
31. They can help to achieve a goal.
32. They can express personal gratitude for something that helped them or their family.
33. They can honor personal achievement.
34. They can focus attention on an agency with which they identify.
35. You can make it easy to make a gift by offering pledge payments, credit cards, etc.
36. You have been thorough in your presentation and they can't see a reason not to give.
37. They respect leaders of the organization.
38. You tell the truth.
39. You listen to their needs and ambitions.
40. You give the donor more than they expect.
41. You don't argue with anyone.
42. You return phone calls.
43. You have every detail of your proposal well in hand.
44. You don't apply too much pressure to give.
45. You develop a relationship with the donor that enhances confidence.

46. You enjoy yourself and fund-raising work and others can see that.
47. You seek the donor's advice on particular aspects of the project's need.
48. You involve the donor's family or company in the project.
49. You speak clearly, with confidence.
50. You know the importance of the donor's time and you use it wisely.
51. Your appearance is professional and appropriate.
52. You are creative in finding ways for the donor to make a gift.
53. Your approach to the project is creative and unique.
54. You position your donor as your mentor or the mentor to others in the organization.
55. You say thanks in informal ways that get the donor's attention.
56. You tell others of the donor's gift and how he or she has made a difference.
57. Your donor knows you work hard and give all you can to the agency.
58. You deal with people as people, not things.
52. You don't garner all the glory, but share success with others in the organization.
60. You know there is no windfall gift — someone, somehow, probably not a fundraiser or an administrator has touched that person's life in a dramatic way.
61. You critically evaluate yourself. What do you do well? What do others do better?
62. You are persistent in your solicitation of the gift.
63. You don't blame others when you're at fault.
64. Your agency or institution works as a team; you work for the greater good.
65. Your ego has not out-distanced your message.
66. You follow up after a request has been made.
67. You're not easily discouraged.

68. When you are told no, you listen to see if you can learn from this temporary setback.
69. You're consistent in the themes of your presentations.
70. You think of the group or organization first, and yourself second.
71. Your agency is focused on its mission and is not trying to be all things to all people.
72. You don't procrastinate about calling prospects and donors.
73. You respond promptly to questions asked by your donor.
74. You establish a personal bond with the prospect.
75. The donor is inspired by the potential of the project.
76. The integrity of the organization strengthens the donor's confidence.
77. The agency pays their bills on time.[3]

Customers or Supporters

Some donors and prospective donors feel nonprofits treat them more as customers than supporters. Nonprofits pay too much attention to selling themselves, these persons say, and not enough attention to describing what they do. Among those who feel this way is Lon M. Burns, retired president of the Southern California Association for Philanthropy. He says charities looking to win his support will consider the following:

"I'm not your customer. I'm not buying anything from you. I choose to support you because I believe in your mission and that you can deal with issues more effectively than I can by myself.

"Please, don't try to persuade me to support you with financial statements in place of information that shows what difference you are making in accomplishing your mission.

"Keep your focus on what you're doing and need to be doing, and don't be too comforted by what you're not doing and not spending.

"Communicate more effectively about what you do, why you do it, and the results of those efforts.

"Be able to go beyond describing what you do to describe what you're *for*. Tell people what happens as a result of your efforts."[4]

He has excellent suggestions, he outlines his needs clearly, and he makes our point — to get gifts churches and other non-profits must pay attention to the needs of donors, whether the needs are spiritual or physical, social or economic, emotional or pragmatic. The principle is the same, whether donors are called contributors, constituents, customers, partners, prospects, givers, supporters, members, or stewards.

Human resources trainer Dale Carnegie created an international business by helping people become successful. "The only way on earth to influence other people," he wrote, "is to talk about what *they* want and show them how to get it."[5]

The Fund-Raising Process

We more easily grasp complex issues when they are reduced to their simplest forms, which is one of the reasons radio and television give us ten-second sound bites for news and top-ten lists for entertainment. Reductions for ease of understanding are not exclusive to modern technology. Such well-known Bible phrases as "The Lord is my shepherd, I shall not want" (Psalms 23:1) and "Believe on the Lord and be saved" (Acts 16:31) give us hope that we will fill in the blanks and come to a more complete understanding at a later time. Stewardship concepts include the buzz words *time, talent, treasure,* and *work, wealth, wisdom,* the precise origins of which have been lost with time and usage.

The Five I's of Fund Raising

So it is with the fund-raising process known as the Five I's: *Identify*, *Investigate*, *Inform*, *Involve*, and *Invite*. Variations of the Five I's have been around since just about anyone can remember. Their precise origins are unknown, although higher education fund-raising executive G. T. "Buck" Smith may have been the first to put the concept into writing.[6]

The fund-raising process is often reduced to three major activities: identify, cultivate, and ask. Regardless of the number, the steps encapsulate the process succinctly, clearly, and relevantly. The process is not one in which you do the first step, stop doing that, move on to the next one, and so forth. Although the steps are in the order they are usually done, the process is ongoing, so that there is a great deal of overlapping and restarting. The pastor, staff, board members, and other volunteers are key persons to be involved in the process, in ways which best meet the prospective donor's needs. The process is specific to an individual prospect — as in a laser beam, not an atomic explosion — whether the prospect is a person or a corporation.

Here is a brief description of the Five I's:

Identify

Identify persons who have a relationship with your church. Begin with those closest to your ministries: members, families, and church friends. Add persons related to a church cemetery program, vendors who do business with your church, bankers, trust officers, and businesses in your church neighborhood who may benefit from the church's location. Current donors are your best prospects for continued and increased giving because they have demonstrated their commitment to give. Create three lists: The Ten Most Wanted (these are the ones with the most money, regardless of whether they will give it), The Next 25, and The Next 100. You will be moving names up and down the lists,

adding names and deleting names, as you learn more about
your prospects, engage them in your ministries, and cultivate their interests in your programs.

Investigate

There are computer programs to help with organizing
information about prospective donors. You can also do it
the old-fashioned way on two sides of a piece of paper, as in
Table 3.1. You need to keep this information only on your
top prospects. Those would be the names on your Ten Most
Wanted and Next 25 lists.

Two cautionary notes: One, the profile information
must be kept strictly confidential. That is, only those persons
who have a need to assemble or use the information should
have access to it. Two, since legal matters might cause the
information to become part of court records, you should
put into the prospect's file only those things you would be
willing to have the prospect see.

Much of what you learn may be anecdotal and that is
okay. You will observe and hear things about which you
may wish to keep notes in a file folder with the Prospect
Profile, along with letters, newspaper clippings, and other
items. These will help you know the interests of the
prospect as well as the prospect's potential and propensity
to give.

In recent years, prospect research has become a major
business subset of fund raising. There are companies which
will search public records to reveal prospects' ownership of
stocks, airplanes, boats, corporate board memberships and
gifts to charities. Major companies providing these services
are listed in each bi-weekly issue of *The Chronicle of
Philanthropy* in its Directory of Services section under the
heading, "Donor Research & Prospect Identification." You
may access the information at the newspaper's website,
http://philanthropy.com. The site provides direct links to
companies.

Table 3.1 Prospect Profile[7]

Side One

Initial Report Prepared By _____ Date _____
Prospect's Name _____
Birth Date _____
Occupation/Title_____
Business Address_____
City_____ State_____ Zip_____
Area Code/Phone_____ Area Code/Fax _____
E-mail_____
Residence_____
City_____ State_____ Zip_____
Area Code/Phone_____ Area Code/Fax _____
E-mail_____
Interests, Hobbies, Affiliations, Comments _____
_____

Spouse's Name_____
Birth Date _____
Occupation/Title_____
Business Address_____
City_____ State_____ Zip_____
Area Code/Phone_____ Area Code/Fax _____
E-mail_____
Interests, Hobbies, Affiliations, Comments _____
Largest Single Gift _____ Estimated Gift Range _____
Possible Deferred/Planned Gift _____
Annuity _____ Trust _____ Will _____ Life Insurance _____
Possible Committee Chair _____
Possible Committee Member _____

Centers of Influence: *Identify persons already committed to the organization who play key roles in influencing the prospect or spouse.*

1._____ 4._____
2._____ 5._____
3._____ 6._____

Agents of Wealth: *Identify those professionals who serve the prospect or spouse to determine the roles they might play in supporting cultivation and solicitation activities.*

Attorney _____ Other_____
Accountant _____ Other_____
Financial Planner _____ Other_____
Broker _____ Other_____

KEY CULTIVATION STRATEGIES	ANTICIPATED TIMING	KEY PLAYERS
_____	_____	_____
_____	_____	_____
_____	_____	_____
_____	_____	_____
_____	_____	_____
_____	_____	_____

Please see other side.

Side Two

Contact Record and Notes

Contact Person _____
Meeting/Date _____
Phone/Date _____
Letter/Date_____
Next Step_____
By Whom and When_____

NOTE: The format on Side Two is repeated several times to fill out the page. The entries direct you to answer the questions: Who was the person who contacted the prospect? Was it a meeting, phone, or letter contact? On what date? What was accomplished? What is the next cultivation activity? Who will do it? By what date?

Inform

Tell the story of your church's successful ministries. Information sharing can be easily woven into existing programs using the pulpit, Sunday bulletins, a pastor's newsletter, family and personal visits, and by personal testimonies of those involved in the ministries. Much of this can be done under the heading of thanking and recognizing donors, which we cover later in this chapter.

Involve

There are many ways to involve prospects. These include asking them to serve on boards and committees, seeking their advice, and asking them to plan or participate in worship services or to direct a program. This is the heart of the fund-raising process: cultivating prospect interest in the church's programs. Unless prospects have a profound sense of ownership in church vision and mission they will never feel motivated to give generously and often. Since most of your gift dollars will come from a handful of donors, you should spend most of your cultivation time with them. The Fund Raising School at Indiana University declares that 60% of the annual fund comes from 10% of donors, 20% comes from 20% of donors, and the remaining 20% comes from 70% of donors.[8] Others have claimed higher ratios, such as 80% of gifts from 20% of donors, and even 90% from 10%.[9]

Invite

As you can see, by the time you get to the point of asking for the gift most of the work has been done. Ask clearly and directly. Mark Driskill, director of development for Adventist World Radio, says: "Speak to the donor in a way that he or she knows what he can do for you — how that donor can take part in your organization's mission." In short, be clear by:

- Considering the donor's interest in supporting your organization.

- Stating your cause directly.

- Making your request perfectly clear.

- Respecting the donor's answer, whether yes or no.

- If the answer is no, evaluate your methods; maybe you can do something differently next time."[10]

Your understanding and application of the fund-raising process will help you determine the needs of prospective donors. If you focus on what is important to the prospect, he or she is more likely to say yes when you ask for the gift.

For more tips on asking for gift, see Chapter Five.

Planning to Say Thank You

Pastors have an opportunity to thank donors more than 52 times each year, yet many do not thank donors even once. Members are hungry to hear this simple courtesy. It can be done from the pulpit during sermons and offertories, in the Sunday bulletin, and by individual phone calls, letters, and visits. Begin your plan to thank donors by changing the offertory prayer from "Thank God for the money" to "Thank God for these wonderful, loving people who have given. We are grateful to them and grateful for their loving response."

Most people like to be recognized, appreciated, and thanked. "Providing a heartfelt and appropriate show of appreciation to those who give to the church," says George Barna, "reinforces people's decisions to give, models Christian graciousness, enhances donors' sense of ownership of the ministry and builds loyalty to the community within the church. The failure to express appreciation undermines the values on which biblical stewardship is based and misses an opportunity to deepen people's commitment to steward-ship."[11]

People Want to be Part of Success

People prefer to be part of successful activities rather than failed ones. They even prefer to be part of perceived successes. A growing church begets growth. A church in a downward trend is very hard to turn around because its lack of dynamic, growth-oriented activities has set it up for fail-ure.

A signal a church could be heading for financial failure is when it prints weekly budget updates in the Sunday bul-letins showing the amount received and the amount still needed. The intention may be to inform and generate giv-ing, but more often these updates generate guilt and portray a negative image, especially for visitors. It is a begging approach to funding ministries rather than a positive, suc-cess-oriented approach. The better use of statements in the Sunday bulletins is to list program successes and thank those who have contributed to the successes.

Use the Bulletin and the Pulpit

In the bulletin and from the pulpit you can declare something like this: "Last month we asked for a new over-head projector for our educational department. We want to thank Fred and Delores Palmer for their gift of a pro-jector in honor of Delores's mother."

Learn to rejoice and thank those who respond by say-ing: "Thanks to each of you who got your pledge in last week. We are pleased to recognize you in today's bulletin," rather than, "If the rest of you will just get your pledges in we can close the campaign." Translated, that last state-ment means, "It will make my life a bunch easier and you won't have to listen to me beg and threaten." Few persons care about the speaker's time and management problems, and fewer care about the mechanics of the campaign. What they care about are the *benefits of the results* of the campaign.

Writing letters and making phone calls to thank donors should be a daily activity. You can never say thank you enough. You should get into the practice of writing or calling every person who has made a special gift over a certain amount. For example, write a thank-you letter to each person who gives more than $100, and telephone each person who gives more than $300. For those who give these amounts every Sunday, write or call them periodically.

Emphasize throughout the year that church ministries continue even when members are not present. After someone has been gone for several weeks and sends a make-up gift, welcome them back with a phone call and thank them for their gift.

The Thank-You Letter

A wonderful opportunity to reduce giving is to mail an impersonal acknowledgment form. Some churches send a computerized monthly or quarterly "record of progress of giving." These statements are often difficult to read and to interpret with their boxes and sections and checked spaces and columns and small print and carbon copies. They meet the need of the church to get the job done efficiently, quickly, and at the least possible expense, but they are a slap in the face to donors. The statements shout, "Your gift is not important and we don't have time to mess with it!" Computers can just as easily produce personally-addressed letters signed by the pastor.

An effective thank-you letter will be short, mention the gift amount, the program to which the donor gave, and the impact of the gift. See Table 3.2. Mention the restricted use of the gift if the donor specified a use. Keep a friendly tone

Table 3.2 Gift Thank-You Letter

Dear Bob and Barbara:

On behalf of the children of Campbell Church I want to thank you for your $500 gift to send two of our youth to Wilderness Camp. Your commitment to Christ and the church will provide a wonderful experience for the children.

I invite you to see the smiling faces of the children on Visitors Day, June 23, as they work, worship, study, and play together. You will especially enjoy the campfire service which over the years has become a life-changing experience for many of them.

Sincerely,

Pastor Bill Bailey

(Handwritten) P.S. If you need a ride on Visitors Day please call me. Several families are pooling rides.

---

and help the donor feel good about making the gift. A hand-written P.S. strengthens ties among the donor, church, and program. It is also a nice way to include a personal touch, such as: "We haven't been fishing in a long time, let's get together," "Congratulations, Barbara, on completing your master's degree," or "Those Pirates are hot — David must be really happy." A note of caution — be careful that your P.S. is not so light-hearted as to dramatically contrast with the theme of your letter. The P.S. statements above, for example, would not be appropriate if your letter was about memorial gifts for a family member.

An example of how strongly members desire atten-tion comes from the pastor whose church averaged 150 worshipers on Sunday mornings and twenty on Sunday nights. One Monday morning she decided to send thank-you letters to those who attended the night before. The next Sunday evening attendance was up. Each week she wrote thank-you letters to those attending Sunday evening services. At the end of a year an average of 100 people were attending each Sunday evening.

If you are thinking, "How can I possibly find the time to pay all this attention to individual donors and prospects?," just remember you are now finding the time to worry about the lack of financial resources to fund ministries.

CHECKLIST FOR SUCCESS

Date Completed

_____ Refer to Robert F. Hartsook's "77 Reasons Why People Give," starting on page 57. If you have not listed the programs and ministries in your church which match his Reasons, do so now.

_____ Prepare your next budget based on programs and ministries to meet the needs of members rather than the needs of the church. Engage area residents and business owners in dialogue to discuss the needs of the community.

_____ Review the fund-raising process to see how you can work the Five I's into your existing programs. Often a slight adjustment in ways of doing things brings dramatic results.

_____ Make a list of what you are doing now to thank and recognize donors. Make a list of what you plan to do. Revisit the lists quarterly and compare the results.

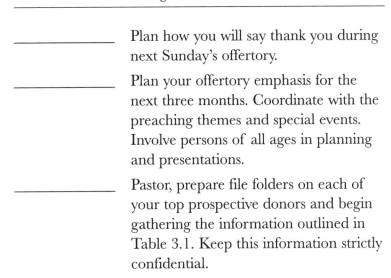

_____ Plan how you will say thank you during next Sunday's offertory.

_____ Plan your offertory emphasis for the next three months. Coordinate with the preaching themes and special events. Involve persons of all ages in planning and presentations.

_____ Pastor, prepare file folders on each of your top prospective donors and begin gathering the information outlined in Table 3.1. Keep this information strictly confidential.

CELEBRATE SUCCESS

List the most valuable ideas you received from this chapter. Set target dates and name persons responsible for implementation, including yourself. List ways to articulate to members and friends of the church the intended or anticipated benefits of the ideas. Create ways to celebrate the successful achievement of the benefits.

NOTES

1 Bruce W. Nelan, "D-Day: Ike's Invasion." *Time*, (6 June 1994, modified 2 June 1995).http://www.pathfinder.com, accesed 8 June 1998. © 1998 Time, Inc. New Media. All rights reserved.

2 In 1991 Congress named the interstate system the Dwight D. Eisenhower System of Interstate and Defense Highways, in recognition of President Eisenhower's initiatives which had resulted in

his signing the interstate highway bill in 1956. Tom Lewis, *Divided Highways* (New York: The Penguin Group, 1997), 98-121, 294.

3   Taken from *FRJ Monthly Portfolio*, November 1997. Edited by Robert F. Hartsook © 1997 Gale Research. All rights reserved. Reproduced by permission.

4   Lon M. Burns, letter, *Chronicle of Philanthropy*, 7 May 1998: 36, 37.

5   Dale Carnegie, *How to Win Friends and Influence People*, Revised Edition (New York: Simon and Schuster, 1981), 62.

6   *Development A Team Approach* (Washington, DC: Council for Advancement of Small Colleges, 1970) 98, in which G. T. "Buck" Smith lists five steps: *identification, information, interest, involvement, investment.* Later, he lists six steps — *identification, information, interest, intervention, involvement, investment* — in *Assuring Your Success: The Cultivation Cycle and the Moves Management Process* (Chicago: Institute for Charitable Giving, n.d.), 2.

7   Adapted from "If You Want a Mega Gift, Create a Mega Plan," *Successful Fund Raising*, July 1995. Stevenson Consultants, Inc., Sioux City, Iowa. Used by permission.

8   The Fund Raising School, Indiana University Center on Philanthropy, Indianapolis.

9   Smith, *Assuring Your Success*, 2.

10 Mark Driskell, "Are You Speaking Clearly?" *The Philanthropic Dollar*, May 1998.

11 George Barna, *How to Increase Giving in Your Church* (Ventura, California: Regal Books, 1997), 122.

4

Stewardship Education and Fund Raising

I'm already working on my budget, programs, and ministries every month, and spending the last couple of months of the year preparing for next year's activities. There is only a limited amount of time on the calendar."

We want to emphasize that fund raising should be attended to on an on-going basis, just as you do with your other programs.

"How do I handle complaints that we talk too much about money?"

The risk of such complaints should be of far less concern than not providing opportunities for members to respond as fully as possible to God's love in all areas of their lives. Money is just one part of stewardship. The ideal is to effectively integrate fund-raising activities with stewardship education, so that there is a seamless delivery.

"How do I go about doing that?"

One way is to look for creative ways to involve more people among many age groups. Churches which are financially sound and spiritually strong involve members in many kinds of stewardship education, including: new-member orientation, estate planning workshops, mailings, sermons, worship services, Sunday school messages, community volunteering, personal testimonies, financial management seminars, individual counseling, videos, brochures, and other training materials, and the offertory.

"That's a plateful of things to do. I'm not sure we can get all of those things going, but we can do some of them. And, by involving more people I can see how we could come up with ideas that would work for us."

Your attitude is right on target. As you make the effort, you likely will discover ways to involve persons who are not now active. Let's see what we can do to help you successfully implement your ideas.

An Integrated Approach

Unplanned learning takes place all around us all the time, from the womb to the grave. It occurs indiscriminately as in the constant bombardment of the sun's rays and involuntarily as in the way we breathe. We observe, process, and mimic the actions of others, saving some information and discarding some for reasons known only in the secrets of our minds. We call up tidbits of our experiences from time to time that impact our decisions to do something or nothing, good or bad, even when we do not realize we are choosing. The effects of unplanned learning can be much like an empty kayak rushing down a raging river — no steering and no goal. You have probably heard it said, "If you don't know where you're going any road will get you there."

Results of Unplanned Learning

Pastors who are uncomfortable talking about money contribute to an unplanned learning environment by not approaching the subject and hoping it never comes up. Church members and the public also contribute to this environment, according to researcher Robert Wuthnow: "In the public at large, fewer than one person in four ever talks about his or her personal finances with close friends. Among church members, only *3 percent* say they ever discuss their finances with fellow church members. And only *4 percent* have ever discussed their finances with a member of the clergy."[1]

The losses are enormous when clergy and members do not talk about money and giving. They include: (1) members who do not understand the Bible's valuable teachings in the wise use of money, (2) pastors who are frustrated at being unable to carry out the full measure of their calling, (3) churches which cannot fund needed ministries for members and for outreach, (4) donor/stewards who respond to God's love at levels below their potential, (5) prospective donor/stewards who do not realize the blessings of personal and spiritual growth from effective financial management.

Money and Personal Values Go Hand in Hand

Some pastors who talk about money tiptoe around the subject with unclear messages, often for fear of alienating their members. This causes misunderstandings and limited responses. The challenge for pastors is to find meaningful ways to teach that money and personal values go hand in hand. "The clergy who are struggling most seriously with questions of money," says Wuthnow, "are often concerned, above all, with getting people to see it in relation to the rest of their lives, especially their values. It is necessary, these clergy are finding, to start at that point because of the prevailing tendency in our culture to compartmentalize money from our values. Two-thirds (68 percent) of the working public, in fact, agree that money is one thing; morals and values are completely separate."[2]

To be most effective, fund-raising activities should not be undertaken without planned stewardship education. We are not going to tell you what to teach regarding stewardship.

That depends on the faith directives of your denomination. We are saying that stewardship education and fund raising should become integral parts of your ministries.

Model Programs

Moses stood on Pisgah Peak and saw the Promised Land. (Deuteronomy 3:27) When we take a Pisgah view of successful stewardship education programs we see that they:

- Are in operation year-round.
- Involve new members.
- Are program oriented.
- Involve team efforts.
- Work with all age groups.
- Include Sunday school, preaching, and literature.
- Emphasize time, talent, and treasure.
- Relate biblical teachings to real life.

You can rate your church's current emphasis on stewardship by responding to the statements in Table 4.1. This model is flexible enough for you to insert specific activities you create to meet the objectives of your program. Rate your program again after one year of activities.

The models in Table 4.2 and Table 4.3 are more specific. They give you plenty of room to be creative and plenty of opportunity to enlist the help of others.

These are growing, dynamic plans to enable purposeful understanding, broad participation, and meaningful response. With programs like these you can increase memberships, operating budgets, and spiritual development. "Rather than simply relying on an annual fund drive, weekly offerings, and then crisis appeals," says seminary

Table 4.1 Profile of A Model Church[3]

Count the number of A's and multiply the total by two. Count the number of P's and add them to the number of A's. Score 24 or more and yours is an above-average church.

	(Circle One) Always	Partially	Seldom
1. The full meaning of stewardship and the way a Christian responds is emphasized throughout the year.	A	P	S
2. Every new member receives orientation about stewardship and is given an opportunity during the first thirty days to make specific commitments in service, attendance, and resources.	A	P	S
3. The church budget reflects special concerns for others in ministry, missions, and giving.	A	P	S
4. There is an approved endowment fund, and a volunteer team works year-round to help people understand and practice the stewardship of accumulated assets through bequests and planned gifts.	A	P	S
5. An educational stewardship program is developed and used annually for Sunday school classes (adults, youth, and children) and all operating units in the church. Information on stewardship resources in the church is shared through literature, videos, and training opportunities.	A	P	S

6. Stewardship is preached throughout the year.	A	P	S
7. Stewardship success is reflected in the willingness of members to serve and to use their talents in a Christian manner. Actions in the church show that people are learning the joys of giving.	A	P	S
8. Funds are available to accomplish the mission and ministries of the church.	A	P	S
9. A model stewardship church will have educational programs that help people understand and make appropriate choices in relation to issues of our natural resources, economic lifestyle, and visions of mission and ministry. There is recognition of the fact that stewardship is a result of spiritual formation and growth.	A	P	S
10. The challenge to tithe is a part of the educational program.	A	P	S

Table 4.2 A One-Year Stewardship Program[4]

Weekly	Place a sentence thought-starter on the subject of percentage giving in the Sunday bulletin.
Monthly	Mention percentage giving from the pulpit in the announcement period or before the offering is received. Use human interest stories from newspapers, magazines, and other sources.
Quarterly	Make a five-to-ten minute presentation on Christian giving to each department of church school from the junior level up. These should be testimonies of personal experiences.

Twice-yearly	Send a letter to every member of the congregation with a pamphlet on tithing enclosed. Pastor delivers a stewardship sermon with emphasis on percentage giving. Enclose a pamphlet with the church bulletin on the date of the sermons.
Yearly	Make a brief presentation to every organization in the church. This could be done on a stewardship emphasis day and could include other program elements.

Table 4.3 A Three-Year Stewardship Program[5]

Year One

January	Begin Program Planning Process
	What is our philosophy of ministry?
	Who are we as a church?
	Where is God calling us in ministry?
May	Recruit Every Member Commitment Committee
	(Fall Funding Program — Every Member Visitation)
Quarterly	1. Stewardship mailing to all members
	2. Stewardship sermons
	(building on commitment and covenant)

Year Two

March	Stewardship Festival
May	Organize for Fall Funding Program
	Recruit committee
	Program: Congregational meetings
September	Conduct Time/Talent/Gifts for Ministry survey
Quarterly	1. Stewardship mailing to all members
	2. Stewardship sermons
	(building on commitment and covenant)

Year Three

January	Emphasis on Wills and Bequests
March	Emphasis on Proportionate Giving and Tithing
May	Organize for Fall Funding Program
	Recruit committee

| November | Christian Financial Management Seminar |
| Year Four | Begin with Year One |

development officer David L. Heetland, "the church which is serious about developing strong stewardship will be equally serious about developing a strong stewardship education program."[6]

A 14-Month Plan

The idea of a 14-month plan is to emphasize that stewardship education and fund raising are on-going activities throughout the year. A simple tool for your 14-month plan is a piece of graph paper. Across the top write the names of 14 months. Down the left side write your activities. Put an X in the square beneath the month and across from the activity to be done that month. Depending on how you write, you may need to tape two pieces of graph paper together. Some software comes with grid options, so that you may construct your plan on a computer.

The 14-month plan in Table 4.4 uses key features of the three model programs and other recommendations.

You may wish to make separate graphs for children, youth, and adults.[7] Involve the leaders and other workers of these departments on the stewardship team to prepare the graphs and the themes, topics, and activities mentioned below. Involve all team members in implementing the plan. It will not be possible to cover all aspects of stewardship education for all age groups every year, so spread your activities over multi-year cycles. Not every activity needs to be done each year, but some activities will be repeated from a previous year.

We suggest using the major stewardship themes of the Bible — giftedness, the environment, service, and finances — every year, one each quarter, or the stewardship

Table 4.4 A 14-Month Plan

	Finances			Giftedness			Environment			Service			Finances	
	Oct	Nov	Dec	Jan	Feb	Mar	Apr	May	Jun	Jul	Aug	Sep	Oct	Nov
Conduct every-member annual campaign and Thanksgiving Sunday celebration	X	X											X	X
Make brief presentation to each church organization on giving	X												X	
Request year-end discretionary giving			X											
Call all major donors		X												
Make presentations to Sunday School classes on giving			X		X			X			X			
Revise the budget			X											
Take a vacation				X										
Approve the final budget				X										
Send a letter on tithing to every member/family and enclose a pamphlet on tithing					X						X			
Announce planned-giving workshop. Name chairperson and committee.							X							
Give stewardship sermon. Enclose stewardship pamphlet in Sunday bulletin.					X					X				
Name committee and chairperson for every-member annual campaign								X						
Plan programs and ministries for next calendar year and draft preliminary budget. Prepare 14-month graph.										X	X			
Conduct planned-giving workshop												X		
Conduct training for every-member annual campaign												X		

Each Week:

Send thank-you letters to donors of $100 or more.
Call on major donors and major donor prospects.
Announce "good news" gifts in Sunday bulletin or from pulpit, to recognize donors.
Announce from the pulpit successful ministries and programs which are achieving their goals. Thank donors and volunteers who support them.
Print a reminder statement in the Sunday bulletin on wills, life insurance, trusts, annuities, real estate, stocks, or bonds. See Table 2.2 in Chapter Two. Use a testimony from a donor who has contributed in one of these ways.
Telephone selected donors and prospects.
Visit potential estate donors.
Phone visitors who made gifts of any size.

themes of your denomination. Select monthly topics for each theme and activities for each topic. Topics for the theme of environment could result in activities of recycling and cleaning up trash from neighborhoods. Topics for the themes of service and giftedness could result in visiting house-bound persons and volunteering at community organizations. Topics for the theme of finances could result in classes on family budget preparation and an estate-planning workshop. Activities can be done within the framework of your existing programs and organizations, including men, women, and youth groups; Sunday school classes; sermons; camps, conferences, and retreats. With imagination and practice you and your stewardship team will find a variety of topics and activities from year to year to keep members informed and busy.

Add as many details to your 14-month plan as you wish in your daily and weekly calendars and in written planning reports. The graph, though, will be the most important management tool for your plan. It is your Pisgah view of the 14 months.

You may start your plan in any month and put the activities into any time period and in any order that fits the life of your church. We chose to start at the end of the calendar year, because these are harvest months when people are in a giving spirit. As much as 20% of your budget may be contributed at the end of the calendar year.

Following are comments on the 14-month plan in Table 4.4.

October - November

Conduct the every-member annual campaign for gifts and pledges to be received during the next calendar year. Use the plan recommended by your denomination or other plan you have chosen. Emphasize financial support for the program and ministry goals previously approved for next year. Finish before Thanksgiving and plan a celebration of success for Thanksgiving Sunday.

December

Ask for year-end discretionary giving. In sermons, offertories, bulletins, and testimonies tell stories of successful programs. Of course, this should be going on all year, but this is an especially good time to do it. Emphasize specific needs as they relate to problems being solved or goals being achieved, such as the following:

- Indian Mission School now enrolls 412 students ages six to seventeen. Your gift provides opportunity for these children and their families to escape from welfare dependency into productive lifestyles.
- We've budgeted for new choir robes, but we do not have the funds to purchase them. The choir is a blessing to our church and to the community. During the past year the choir was invited to sing at eight other churches, four community organizations, and three nursing homes. Your gift will help continue and strengthen these blessings.
- The church van needs new tires. The van is the only transportation available to frail elderly for church attendance and shopping. We have put 92,000 miles on the van in helping forty-one elderly persons since acquiring the van three years ago. Your generosity has made this ministry possible and we know you would like to keep it going.
- We're looking for four sponsors to purchase Sunday School literature, one sponsor for each quarter of next year. Our Sunday School has grown by 13% in the past four years.

Make a list of people who have the ability and disposition to give. Call them and meet with them individually to ask them to give a second gift and allow you to thank them publicly. Similarly, ask for and announce matching gifts:

"We have a donor who will match dollar-for-dollar the amount of additional gifts over $250 for this ministry. "

"We have a donor who will pay the last 50% to complete this program."

Invite persons to pre-pay next year's pledges to help meet this year's budget. This will improve your cash flow for this year, enable an option for donors which may meet their needs, and cause donors to consider giving more next year.

People respond to leadership and to opportunities for success. Rejoice with your members when together you have met your goals. If your goals are not reached, rejoice in what has been positively accomplished. Evaluate whether you took on more than members were willing to support, or whether you could have done more to enable additional giving.

January - February

This is an excellent time to take a vacation. It is time to renew your spiritual life and celebrate with your family. Part of good stewardship is being a good steward over your mental attitude and your family morale. The tension is off, so enjoy! When you return, evaluate last year's ministries and financial responses, and consider adjustments.

March - April

Announce the planned-giving workshop for September and schedule reminder announcements. Select a committee and a chairperson. Be sure the chairperson has made an estate plan that includes your church. Mail information on the workshop to every member/family. Arrange for reservations to confirm attendance.

May - June

Appoint the committee for the every-member annual campaign to be conducted in the fall. Select a chairperson who is one of your top donors. Many excellent campaign guidelines are available from denominations and intra-denominational church publishers. Check with your national headquarters and your local bookstore.

July - August

Plan your programs and ministries for the next calendar year. Yes, this is the time to do it, not on December 31! Use the plans to develop a tentative budget and to establish dollar goals for the every-member annual campaign. Think programs and ministries first, then budget.

Get out the graph paper and start writing. Put your completed graph into a three-ring binder or file folder and mark it for the current year. Mark another binder or folder for next year. In both, plan to store ideas for fund raisers, stewardship sermons, offertories, worship themes, names of volunteers, and prospective leadership donors. You now have a management tool to meet the needs of funding ministries that will not be limited by an unbalanced budget.

Schedule sermon topics and offertory themes. Special days can become memorial or tribute days. People like to remember and say thank you at Mother's Day, Father's Day, Memorial Day, Labor Day, Veterans Day, Thanksgiving, and so forth. Weave into your sermons the theology of stewardship, especially in conjunction with the ecclesiastical calendar of Lent, Pentecost, Easter, and others.

Church departments will want to have fund-raising activities, such as a car wash, chili supper, bike ride, or candy sale. Schedule these as far in advance as possible and encourage departments to broaden their lists of possible volunteers and participants. Income from a fund-raising activity often goes to the department sponsoring the activity for unbudgeted needs. It can also help fund a budgeted program or ministry.

September

Conduct the planned-giving workshop. Finish plans for the every-member annual campaign, conduct training, and announce the dollar goal.

October - November

Conduct the every-member annual campaign, finishing with a celebration on Thanksgiving Sunday.

December

Ask for year-end discretionary giving. Celebrate your successes.

Seasonal appeals other than at Christmas or other traditional times may meet the needs of some donors. Try asking for gifts in December and in May to purchase religious education materials for the coming quarter or year. In May, September, November, and December emphasize gifts of real estate. April and October are excellent times to ask for gifts for landscaping of church property. Put these and other asking opportunities you may think of on your 14-month graph as planning reminders.

———————

This plan is only a starting point. Your 14-month plan for stewardship education and fund raising should speak directly to the vision and mission of your church. Even after your plan is written, be prepared to make adjustments to fit changing circumstances. As well, vary the schedule and activities from year to year to maintain freshness, sustain interest, and increase involvement.

CHECKLIST FOR SUCCESS

Date Completed

_____   Write an honest evaluation of the stewardship education level of your congregation. With the help of other donor/stewards, develop a stewardship education program to fit your congregation's needs. If skills to do this are lacking in your congregation, seek help from your denominational headquarters, consultants, or a local or nearby Bible college or seminary. Visit a Christian book store for self-directed study materials.

_____   Begin work on your 14-month plan and graph. Start with any month, any activity, in any order.

_____   If you do not have a stewardship committee or a stewardship team, now is an excellent time to organize one. Choose representatives from your board, Sunday School classes, administrative leadership, general membership, and other key groups. Be sure all are donors, or ask them to agree to become donors if they agree to serve. Meet with this group at least bi-monthly to hear their advice, make plans, and enlist their volunteer leadership in specific projects.

_____   List the names of persons with demonstrated dispositions to give and the ability to give more. How will you help them want to give more?

_____   Make files for clippings and notes on the following subjects: Stewardship of Environment, Stewardship of Money, Stewardship of Giftedness, and Stewardship of Service.

_____   Identify two persons each week to thank during the Sunday service. List as many different ways to say thank you as you can and use them. Keep revising the list throughout the year. A thank-you can be for a gift, a leadership role, volunteer efforts, a thoughtful testimony, a caring gesture, and other actions. It can be public or private.

_____   Change the wording of your gift thank-you letters at least three times yearly.

CELEBRATE SUCCESS

List the most valuable ideas you received from this chapter. Set target dates and name persons responsible for implementation, including yourself. List ways to articulate to members and friends of the church the intended or anticipated benefits of the ideas. Create ways to celebrate the successful achievement of the benefits.

NOTES

1   Robert Wuthnow, *The Crisis in the Churches: Spiritual Malaise, Fiscal Woe* (New York: Oxford University Press, 1997), 141.

2   Wuthnow, 148.

3   Jim Tarr in Donald W. Joiner and Norma Wimberly, Editors, *The Abingdon Guide to Funding Ministry, Vol. 1* (Nashville: Abingdon Press, 1995), 95. Used by permission.

4   Charlie W. Shedd, *How to Develop A Tithing Church* (Nashville: Abingdon Press, 1961), 45-47. Used by permission.

5   Donald W. Joiner in Joiner and Wimberly, 103. Used by permission.

6   David L. Heetland, *Fundamentals of Fund Raising* (Nashville: Discipleship Resources, 1989), 55.

7   Paul K. Ritchie in Joiner and Wimberly, 100-102.

5

Asking for the Big Gift

I'm beginning to feel pretty good about this business of fund raising."
We're glad to hear that. In what way?

"Things seem to be coming together, even though there is a lot to track. Much of what you recommend is common sense, such as paying attention to the needs of donors and planning for fund raising. Fund raising doesn't just happen, you have to decide to make it happen."

As in accepting Jesus Christ.

"Right. And, after we have decided to accept the Lord, He expects us to get on with His work, not sit around and twiddle our thumbs. Doing the Lord's work takes money and knowing how to raise the money helps us move forward His agenda."

It sounds as though you have packed your parachute, gone up in the airplane and are about ready for the big jump.

"That's a pretty good description of me right now."

The big jump is asking for the big gift. Are you ready?

"Let's do it!"

What Wealthy People Are Really Like

One of America's first major philanthropists was Andrew Carnegie, born in Scotland. He made his fortune in

the steel business in the mid-to-late 1800s. When he sold his
business to United States Steel in 1901 he was able to give
five million dollars to employees for their pension and benefit fund.[1] At five per-cent interest compounded annually,
that would be more than $567 million in 1998.

Carnegie felt strongly about "the proper administration
of wealth, that the ties of brotherhood may still bind
together the rich and poor in harmonious relationship,"[2] as
he wrote in his 1889 essay on wealth. He believed the rich
should return "their surplus wealth to the mass of their fel-
lows in the forms best calculated to do them lasting good."[3]
He declared the best fields for philanthropy to be higher
education, libraries, hospitals, parks, concert halls, public
swimming pools, and churches.[4] Hundreds of projects
throughout the United States are named for him as testament to his commitment and generosity.

Carnegie did not limit his gospel to the wealthy. "It is
not the privilege, however, of millionaires alone to work for
or aid measures which are certain to benefit the community," he wrote. "Every one who has but a small surplus
above his moderate wants may share this privilege with his
richer brothers, and those without surplus can give at least
a part of their time, which is usually as important as funds,
and often more so."[5]

Wealthy persons are not always as high profile as
Andrew Carnegie, or today's Warren Buffett and Bill Gates.
Studies of wealthy persons have included those with
invested assets of more than one million dollars or who
made charitable gifts of more than one million dollars.
Studies have also included those we might think of as ordinary working people — secretaries, teachers, and clerks
among them — who silently accumulated wealth. Some key
characteristics of wealthy donors have emerged from this
body of research, as shown in Table 5.1.

Stories abound of the silent wealthy who gave small gifts
to churches or other nonprofits over many years then surprised the organizations late in their lives with large gifts or
with large estate gifts.

Table 5.1 Key Characteristics of Wealthy Donors

They enjoy:

1. Individual attention and relationship building.

2. Seeing the benefits of their gifts.

3. Having their giving needs met, whether personal, social, or financial.

4. The freedom of being able to help others.

5. Appropriate recognition and thanks.

They are concerned about:

1. Keeping their wealth from going to big government.

2. An image that wealthy persons can do it all.

3. Organizations which mismanage or misdirect financial resources.

They are motivated to give money and volunteer because they:

1. Are already involved with the organization.

2. Were asked, usually by a peer.

3. Feel their gifts can make a difference.

4. See the support of other individuals and organizations.

5. Want to be part of a successful team effort.

On the other hand, Thomas J. Stanley and William D. Danko — who have studied wealthy people for more than twenty years — conclude that, among America's 3.5 million millionaires, most are tightwads. Most also own ordinary businesses, such as mobile-home parks and paving companies, made it on their own without an inheritance, live well below their means in neighborhoods where there are three times more non-millionaires than millionaires, drive American-made cars not of the current model year, are college graduates, and make their own investment decisions.[6]

How Big is A Big Gift?

There is nothing precise about the definition of big. Scientists consider our sun to be a small star, yet 1.3 million earths could fit inside it. Jonah was swallowed by a big fish and Gulliver was a giant among the Lilliputians.

What is considered to be a big gift varies among churches, depending on the number of members and their affluence. We have found many churches and other non-profits use $5,000 or $10,000 as the starting point for big gifts. CEOs of some nonprofits become actively involved in gift cultivation and solicitation only for prospective gifts of $25,000 or more. Higher education institutions with sophisticated and highly experienced fund development operations, such as Stanford University and Harvard University, have teams working exclusively on securing gifts of one million dollars or more.

To help you determine what a big gift is for your church consider the differences between the *nature* of annual gifts and major gifts, as shown in Table 5.2. Annual gifts are usually small. Decisions on how much to give and when are often made at the moment of asking. Major gifts are usually larger than annual gifts. The decision-making process may take months or years and involve the prospect's family, accountant, lawyer, insurance agent, and stock broker.

"There should be no limit to the amount of money that a church could spend in the Lord's work," says consultant Ashley Hale. "But to receive big money, you must have big plans, work on fund raising all year around, and ask for big gifts."[8]

There are three key steps to asking for the big gift: preparation, the asking interview, and follow-up. As we go through these steps we will suggest what to say and what not to say and explain what the prospects may really mean when they hesitate or say no. If your church is in an endowment or capital campaign there should be solicitation training sessions presented by the campaign consultant, usually

Table 5.2 Differences Between Annual Gifts and Major Gifts[7]

Annual Gifts	*Major Gifts*
1. Prospect is treated more as a customer	Prospect is treated as an investor/shareholder.
2. You are working your agenda and deadline.	You are working with the prospect's agenda and timeline.
3. Focus is on the organization's needs.	Focus is on the prospective donor's needs.
4. Gifts are made regularly (monthly, annually, etc.) at usually less than $10,000.	Often a one-time "stretch gift" of significant financial resources
5. Prospects are asked by letter or telephone.	Prospects are asked face-to-face.
6. Ask, negotiate, close sequence is a simultaneous transaction.	Ask, negotiate, close sequence may take several meetings over a period of months or years.
7. Gifts are usually given in cash from current income.	Gifts are often given in appreciated assets from capital resources.
8. Gifts are solicited on a cyclical basis and against the organization's short-term goals.	Gifts are solicited with the donor's financial circumstances in mind and can often take months or years to complete.
9. The volunteer or staff person usually works alone to close his or her own solicitation.	A team approach among volunteers, staff and CEO is used to contact, cultivate, and solicit prospects.
10. Gifts are usually for unrestricted purposes.	Gifts are almost always restricted to a specific donor request.

at the church. The techniques covered in this chapter are applicable for asking situations anytime, regardless of whether you are in a campaign.

Preparation

The most important part of asking for the big gift is that the right person does the asking. This could be the pastor, a staff person, a volunteer, or professional counsel. The best way to determine who should ask is to answer the question: "To whom can the prospect not say no?" Your success is directly related to the answer. Unlike for smaller gift prospects, who can be asked by any number of dedicated but inexperienced people, you want to put in front of big-gift prospects the person or persons who cannot possibly be turned down.

Askers must set an example by making their own gifts. "When asked for a major contribution," says businessman Michael Bloomberg, "if I'm interested in the cause, my first question to the solicitor is, 'What did the organization's board members and you personally give?' If you and they don't support the cause, maybe it doesn't deserve my help."[9] As an asker you will be more sincere and convincing if you are a donor. You will generate momentum and credibility, and your gift will help achieve the dollar goal. This does not mean you must give $25,000 if that is what you are asking of the prospect. It does mean you must be among the first persons in your church to make a gift or pledge to the program for which you are soliciting gifts, and your gift must be appropriate to your circumstances. It is wonderful to be able to say to the prospect, "I have made my commitment, and I invite you to join with me and others to help make this program a success."

Training as Part of Preparation

Getting the gift also depends a great deal on your knowledge of the program. See Chapter Two on the types of fund-raising programs and Chapter Three on planning. Review all aspects of the fund program your church is doing so that you may be prepared to the best of your ability to respond to the prospect's questions.

If your church has engaged fund-raising counsel, the consultant should conduct training sessions for volunteer askers. If training by the consultant is not available, check with the nearest chapter of the National Society of Fund Raising Executives for names of chapter members who may be willing to provide training guidelines, or even conduct the training, at no cost. Sometimes, chapters take on a project such as this as a mentoring activity. Other options include developing training sessions using the best available volunteer talent in your local church, or enlisting the help of your denomination's headquarters staff.

Training topics should include such things as:

- Program goals and objectives
- Overview of the fund-raising process
- Printed materials and how to use them
- Organizational structure, including teams and reporting methods
- Telephone manners and techniques
- Methods of asking for the gift
- Assignment of prospects to askers

Making the Appointment

The next part of your preparation is to telephone the prospect for an appointment. Most people appreciate this courtesy. In most cases you are calling someone you know and who is expecting your call. The prospect has already received a great deal of information regarding the program as the result of planning sessions, church meetings, announcements from the pulpit, distribution of printed materials, committee assignments, training workshops, and so forth. The program is not something the prospect is hearing about for the very first time when you call.

Your purpose in calling is to make an appointment, not to ask for the gift. You might say something like this: "Hi, this is Mary Johnson. I'm following up on the letter you received from our campaign chair (or something similar that ties the call to the campaign). I'm wondering when we could get together to discuss your gift. What is your schedule like this week or next week?" Do not stop speaking after you say "discuss your gift." Move quickly to the next statement of the prospect's schedule. This keeps the focus of your call on the appointment and not the gift. If you stop after "discuss your gift" the prospect may give you a gift decision right then and there. A gift commitment on the phone will most likely be for a smaller amount than if you asked for it face-to-face.

Do not try to answer too many questions on the phone. Your objective is get an appointment. Set a specific time and place for the appointment. You could say something like: "Is morning or afternoon better for you?" "Do you prefer your office or your home?" "Will your spouse (use his or her name) be joining us?"

State that the appointment will take less than 20 minutes, then repeat the appointment time and place. Fill out an appointment information card while you are talking. See Table 5.3. Ask for directions if you are not familiar with the appointment place and write the directions on the appointment card. If another asker will be going with you be sure to tell the prospect at this time. Say "thank you" and you are done. Immediately after hanging up mark your calendar. Take your appointment cards with you on the days you make your calls.

Table 5.3 Appointment Information Card

Side One

Appointment Date _____ Time _____

Location _____

Directions _____

Prospect's Name _____

Spouse's Name _____

Job Title/Employer _____

Office Phone _____ Home Phone_____

Estimated Gift Range _____ Possible Estate Gift _____

Prospect would ask others to give: Yes   No
(If yes, please list names on other side.)

Prospect would work in other ways: Yes   No
(If yes, please list ways on other side.)

See notes on other side

Asker's Signature _____

Side Two

*After your appointment, please attach the signed
pledge card and return in the envelope provided. Thank you.*

Notes_____

_____

_____

_____

_____

_____

MATERIALS CHECKLIST

Please bring the following items to your appointment as needed:

Case Statement	New Sanctuary Brochure
Prayer Center Brochure	Pledge Card
Wills Booklet	Community Partners Brochure
Pen, Pencil, Notepad	New Ministries Booklet
Endowment Funds Brochure	

After the Phone Call

A nice personal touch is to send a handwritten note to the prospect confirming the appointment. If your program has ample volunteer or paid help the person designated can send a typewritten confirmation over your signature. A confirmation note is not necessary if the appointment is just two or three days away. You may arrive before the note.

Shortly before you arrive for the appointment rehearse what you are going to say to the prospect. Say the words over and over, out loud. Visualize yourself going into the prospect's home or office, standing here, sitting there, saying specific words. This visualization technique is used by many successful athletes and sales people. If you are calling on the prospect with a partner, you should rehearse together, so both know what points each will be covering. You can rehearse in the car, over the phone, or at the place you meet just before seeing the prospect. Decide who will make the ask and at approximately what point in the interview.

Making calls in pairs has advantages for askers and prospects. The askers are able to support each other's testimony, share in assessing how the interviews worked, and are strengthened by companionship. Prospects place greater importance on the ask and their resistance is reduced.

The Asking Interview

When you are in front of the prospect keep small talk to a minimum, just a couple of minutes. Comment on something positive you know about the prospect, such as an item that may have appeared recently in the newspaper, a picture on the wall that confirms the prospect's interest in sports or community service, or something you have in common.

Share the statement of support for your program, such as a brochure or booklet, pointing out key areas in which you know the prospect is interested. Be sure to bring a brochure for each person who will be in the interview so all can be directed to the same message at the same time, including your partner. Testify to your first-hand knowledge of the benefits of the church's program. Do not say, "The church *needs* this building program." Instead, say, "Increasing the size of the sanctuary will enable 100 more persons to worship regularly." Or, "The newly paved and enlarged parking lot will hold fifty more cars and worshipers will no longer have to stumble in loose gravel and potholes." Or, "This program will involve twenty-five teenagers each week in activities that will help keep them from getting into trouble on the streets." Talk about the *benefits* of your program to those you serve and desire to serve, including the prospect, and how the prospect's participation will help the benefits to occur. Be sure your comments are directed toward the prospect's interests. Be proud you are providing an opportunity for the prospect to advance the mission of your church.

Three Key Phrases

Ask for the gift. That is why you are there. Believe it or not, many people skip over this part. They may stumble with something non-committing, such as, "Will you help us please?" Or, "Well, what do you think?" Or, "Anything you can give will be appreciated."

There are three phrases that will serve you well in any gift-asking situation. Memorize these and you will always be able to ask for money from anyone, for any program, anytime and anywhere. Next to having the right person ask for the gift, these phrases are the most important thing you take with you to the interview. Notice the phrases are open-ended.

Phrase #1. "We are calling on persons who may be interested in giving $10,000 or more. Where do you see your participation?" This is a compliment to the prospect. The prospect now knows you have not come for anything smaller, and that there are others you are going to ask for the same amount. The prospect feels valued at being part of a team effort. And, you have given the prospect an opportunity to decide what giving level is in the prospect's best interests.

Phrase #2. "We were wondering whether you could consider a gift of $50,000 over five years." This is a statement, not a question. It enables the prospect to *consider* an appropriate response rather than *requiring* a specific response. It also opens the door for completing a pledge over a period of time, which may be more attractive to the prospect than writing a check for the full amount today.

Phrase #3. Hand the prospect a chart of giving levels required for the program to be successful, similar to Table 5.4. Ask the prospect to look at the left-hand side, then beginning at the highest level, thumb down the chart and say, "We have a gift in this first range, and in this range, and this range. In this next range we are looking for three gifts. We were wondering whether you could consider being one of them." Although you have not specified a dollar amount, the prospect clearly sees what you expect. Thumbing down the chart declares the program is gaining support, focuses the prospect's attention on a higher amount, and shows the prospect would not be alone at that gift level.

Body Language

Lean forward slightly and look directly at the prospect when making the ask. Speak confidently and smile gently, expecting the prospect to respond favorably. After you have asked for the gift, be silent. Do not say anything. The silence may go on for several seconds. It only seems like hours. Let the prospect be the first to speak. If you let the prospect break the silence you have a much better chance of securing the gift. We guarantee if you do not speak, the prospect will.

Table 5.4 Levels of Giving

Standard of Giving to Secure $1,000,000

Amount of Gift	Number Needed	Category Total	Totals
$250,000 and above	1	$ 250,000	$ 250,000
100,000 to 249,999	1	100,000	350,000
75,000 to 99,999	3	225,000	575,000
50,000 to 74,999	3	150,000	725,000
25,000 to 49,999	6	150,000	875,000
10,000 to 24,999	6	60,000	935,000
5,000 to 9,999	6	30,000	965,000
1,000 to 4,999	10	10,000	975,000
Many Gifts Under 1,000		25,000	$1,000,000

Note the top five gifts make up more than one-half the goal. The contents of a giving chart depend on the potential in your church. Professional counsel or a volunteer fund-raising executive can help you prepare a chart for your programs.

Use the third person "we" even if you are alone. It is a softer approach than the first person "I" and subtly indicates many persons are involved with the program. Do not say, "We have you down for this amount." Or, "Brother Edwards said you could give this much." Do not reveal the amount others have given or pledged unless you have their permission.

With practice you will be able to ask for the gift with effortless assurance and with a great deal of personal satisfaction at your results. You will be exhilarated to the point of walking on air when the prospect says, "Yes, I will do that."

When the Prospect Hesitates

Very seldom will prospects say the word "no" after being asked for the gift. If they are not prepared to say yes at this point they may hesitate and say they want to think it over or check with their spouse or board of directors. This is only natural. Prospects used to dealing with large amounts of money for business or investment purposes usually do not make financial decisions without a lot of thought. You should be respectful of their willingness to consider your proposal. After your prospect has said he or she wants to think it over, you could say, "What can we do to help you consider a favorable response?" Then, be silent again. If the prospect wants a few days to make a decision then say, "When would be the best time to get back to you?" and mark your calendar.

If the prospect says yes to an amount you feel is far below his or her capabilities, you may try to increase the amount. Be careful to use a tenderness of tone that does not offend when doing this. For example, you asked for a gift of $50,000 and the prospect commits to $5,000. You could say, "That's wonderful. Many persons have made commitments at that level and we appreciate it very much. We were wondering whether you could consider $5,000 a year for five years." Be silent. If the prospect says yes, begin filling out the pledge card. If the prospect sticks with his or her lowered commitment, state your pleasure at the amount and begin filling out the pledge card.

Be Flexible

The prospect's commitment should fit the prospect's needs and desires, not some hard and fast rules that can never be adjusted. You want to say *yes*. Here are some common reasons prospects hesitate or say no and what your response could be:

The ask amount is too high. "What amount would best fit your situation?"

The pledge period is not satisfactory. "Over what period would you like to fulfill your pledge?" "Would you prefer reminders annually, semi-annually, or quarterly?" "When would you like to start?"

The method of giving is not acceptable. "You do not have to give any cash today. Part of your gift could be in cash over a period of several years and part could be from your estate, such as life insurance or a bequest. What would work best for you?"

The purpose does not fit the prospect's needs. "Would you prefer to designate your gift to _____ or would you prefer your gift be used where the need is greatest?"

The Pledge Card

Keep the pledge card out of sight until a commitment is made. Do not leave the pledge card with the prospect as it weakens the possibility of getting a gift and has the effect of reducing the size of the gift. When filling out the card be sure to get the prospect's correct home and office address, and home phone and office phone. Find out at which address the prospect prefers to receive friendly reminders. Ask the prospect to sign the card. Say that a formal acknowledgment will be mailed. Be sure to say thank you.

Now is an excellent time to discuss an estate gift if it did come up during the interview. You could say, "Do you have the church in your will?" Or, "Have you considered giving a paid-up life insurance policy or creating a trust or annuity?" Do not try to explain the complexities of these or other charitable estate gifts at this time unless you are knowledgeable of them. You are just opening doors. Suggest sending some information or having an expert contact the prospect. Make a note of the prospect's response on your appointment card.

Follow Up

Send a handwritten note to the prospect within three days after your interview. If a pledge or gift was received in the interview thank the donor and state that a formal letter of acknowledgment will be sent soon. If no pledge or gift was received state you have marked your calendar for the date of a follow-up visit. Mention a special item of interest the donor discussed, such as, "We appreciate your interest in the endowment fund and know you will feel good about strengthening it." Or, "Best wishes with your presentation at the national workshop next month."

Turn in all of your interview notes, pledge cards, and other materials for tracking and reporting purposes according to the procedures your church has established. These may be procedures established especially for a campaign or they may be procedures your church uses all of the time. Be sure the church's estate planning officer or other designated person gets the information regarding the prospect's interest in wills, trusts, annuities, or life insurance.

It is important to recognize donors for their gifts. The kinds of recognition vary greatly, from a list of donors in a booklet or on wall plaques to naming pews, rooms, or other structures. An announcement from the pulpit asking a key donor to stand and receive applause — with the donor's prior approval — can be effective. Gift recognitions should not be done haphazardly. They should be written into your gift acceptance guidelines and reviewed for each new fundraising program. See Chapter Six on how to prepare gift acceptance guidelines.

Avoid giving coffee mugs, ball caps, letter openers, key chains, and the like. There may be a place for these in other church activities, but not in recognizing major donors.

CHECKLIST FOR SUCCESS

Date Completed

_____   Make a list of the wealthy donors in
                    your congregation, using the criteria of
                    Thomas J. Stanley and William D.

Table 5.5 Pledge Card

"Responding to God's Love"
The Campaign for Community Outreach

Church of the Good Shepherd

Yes, I want to support the Campaign for Community Outreach.
I/we pledge the sum of _____ over _____ years, as follows:
Amount enclosed _____. Balance of _____ to be paid in equal
installments ❑Annually ❑Semi-Annually ❑Quarterly
starting on or about _____.
    Please send friendly reminders to my ___ home ___ office.
Name _____
Spouse's Name _____
Home Address _____
City _____ *State* _____ *Zip* _____
Home Phone _____
Company Name _____
City _____ *State* _____ *Zip* _____
Company Phone _____

Signature _____ *Date*_____

I am interested in knowing more about the following kinds of gifts:
(Check as many as you wish)
    ❑Stocks and Bonds   ❑Real Estate   ❑Life Insurance
    ❑Bequest   ❑An Income for Life Through Trusts and Annuities
    ❑I have made arrangements for a gift to the Church in my will.

    Note: A copy of the completed pledge card should be
included with the acknowledgment letter. The asker should initial the pledge card before turning it in.

_____ Danko at the beginning of this chapter.
List things you will do to meet their
needs and involve them in church life.

_____   Pastor, list the names of those in your congregation who gave $5,000 or more during the past year, as well as those who gave one large annual gift rather than several smaller gifts. Did you thank them? Did you recognize them? What potential is there for additional gifts from them? List strategies for securing additional gifts from them, such as enlisting their help in cultivating and asking others for gifts.

_____   Pastor, review the giving records of congregational department heads and other leaders. Are all of them donors? List strategies for asking for their gifts or for upgrading their giving levels.

_____   Review your fund-raising printed materials and update if necessary. Be sure materials are of the highest quality text, layout, and printing. Be sure materials you share with wealthy persons speak their language and speak to their needs, especially regarding investments and charitable estate planning.

_____   Pastor, develop a list of prospective estate donors from among your members and close church friends. Develop a plan to regularly send them informational mailings. Invite selected prospective estate donors and estate donors to become members of your stewardship team. They could chair the committees for your every-member annual campaign or planned-giving workshop, or have other roles in those programs.

_____   Consider adding the statement,
"Consider leaving the congregation in
your will," to the bottom of church
stationary or on the outside flap of the
carrier envelope.

CELEBRATE SUCCESS

List the most valuable ideas you received from this chapter. Set target dates and name persons responsible for implementation, including yourself. List ways to articulate to members and friends of the church the intended or anticipated benefits of the ideas. Create ways to celebrate the successful achievement of the benefits.

NOTES

_____

1   From *The Gospel of Wealth and Other Timely Essays*, Edward C.
    Kirkland, Editor (Cambridge: Belknap Press of Harvard
    University Press, 1962), xxii.
2   Carnegie, 14.
3   Carnegie, 28.
4   Carnegie, 32-46.
5   Carnegie, 47.
6   Thomas J. Stanley and William D. Danko, *The Millionaire Next
    Door: The Surprising Secrets of America's Wealthy* (Atlanta: Longstreet
    Press, 1996), 8-11.
7. Developed by William F. Dailey, Paul V. Edwards, Ernest W.
    Wood. © 1990 The Russ Reid Company and Paul V. Edwards.
    Used by permission.

8   Ashley Hale, *The Lost Art of Church Fund Raising* (Chicago: Precept Press, 1993), 45.

9   Michael Bloomberg, *Bloomberg by Bloomberg* (New York: John Wiley & Sons, 1997), 234.

6
Doing the Right Thing — Issues of Ethics and Accountability

I'm a little concerned you think our church members intentionally would take advantage of the trust we have for each other or in any way abuse the finances of the church."

We feel strongly that precautionary measures should be in place.

"Precautionary for what? We're just good, honest people trying to do the Lord's work."

We certainly can accept that. We also know whenever people handle or control money belonging to someone else there can be temptation. Personal worries over financial matters have caused some members of other churches to illegally divert church funds in order to get themselves out of trouble.

"That would never happen in our church."

You are probably right. Rather than adding to what are already the many temptations of life by not taking *any* precautions, we think it would be much better to have a system fair to all members, and that all members understand and appreciate. That way, the system works, taking the burden off individual decision making.

"What does that have to do with fund raising?"

It is important to have systems in place for handling regular offerings as well as money from fund-raising programs. Each has its own special challenges of management and accountability.

"That sounds like it is going to cost our church more money, take more time, and involve more people."

That may very well be. We would advise you to look at your particular situation and determine how much of a system you should put into place to meet your needs. A reminder, though, that members in smaller churches are just as susceptible to temptations as those in larger ones.

"Can I reserve judgment on our needs until I see what you propose?"

Fair enough.

The Edge of Ethics

The following story has been around for a long time. You may have heard it.

The night before an important exam, four college students decided to party rather than study. The next day they showed up for class when the exam was nearly over. They had smeared grease on their hands and told the professor they were late because they had to fix a flat tire on their car. "Could you please schedule us to take the test later?" they asked. The professor agreed and set the test for the next week. The students were delighted with the success of their fakery. Over the next few days they studied and on test day felt they were ready. The professor placed each student alone in separate classrooms. The first question was worth five points and the students thought it was quite easy. The second question was worth 95 points and read, "Which tire?"

Most of us would agree the boys did wrong, regardless of the outcome of the test. Humorous stories like this illustrate that lies, deceits, and contrivances may temporarily get us out of a jam, but can trip us up later. The following story is not humorous. It illustrates a common problem regarding ethical behavior, about which not everyone agrees as to the appropriate solution.

The Pastor and the Chairman

It was January 18 and the church's financial records for the previous year were in the process of being closed. The chairman of the church board came into the pastor's office and handed him a check in the amount of $10,000. The check was dated December 31. "The check has been sitting on my desk while we were vacationing in the Caribbean," said the chairman. "I'm sorry I didn't get it to you sooner. Just show it as a gift for last year so I can get the tax deduction."

Was the chairman telling a lie? Was he trying to deceive the pastor? Was his story contrived? The pastor knew the IRS rule on end-of-the-year gifts: a check dated on or before December 31 that arrives at the church in an envelope postmarked on or before December 31 may be claimed as a deduction for the year in which the check is written. Should the pastor accept the check with gratitude or risk losing a big gift and offending the donor? Clearly, the pastor was being tempted, but he was up to the challenge. He did the right thing by convincing the chairman to write a new check with a current date.

Some Gifts May Have to be Turned Down

It may not always be in the best interest of your church to accept every gift offered. Consider the following scenarios:

- A board member wants to give a five-figure gift to create a program that is not part of your vision or mission.

- A volunteer is raising money for a program not authorized by your board, even though it is an important and needed program.

- A handful of members want to start a fund restricted to their narrow interests with their gifts of $25 each. You know there is not enough interest throughout the church to support the fund's growth nor to manage the program.

- An organization that exploits women offers a major gift to help fund your program for abused women and children.

- A former member who has moved away says he will give a Rolls Royce to auction off as a fund raiser. He fails to disclose the car has not been cleaned up nor repaired since being in a hurricane.

- A member wants to give some land for construction of a new church building. In return he wants a receipt for an amount unrealistically higher than the land's value.

"Churches that are not guided by *policies* and *procedures* are vulnerable to being misguided by *personalities*," says pastor Richard L. Bergstrom[1]

The Many Faces of Ethics

The literature of religion and philosophy is rich with information on ethical behavior and considerable research is available on ethical standards of business and government. "Nevertheless, almost no research exists on the ethics of philanthropy," says management professor Michael

O'Neill, "although funders and fund raisers have practiced or violated ethical principles, stated or unstated, for millennia."[2] He says a major reason so little research is available is that philanthropy as a field of study is only about 20 years old.

The Golden Rule (Luke 7:12) is an often-stated standard for ethical behavior. Just about everyone knows it even though we do not always practice it: treat others the way you would like to be treated. The Golden Rule has found its way into an incalculable number of mission statements of businesses and nonprofits in many different forms, often as expressions of quality and customer service. One of the most recognized is Rotary International's four-way test in all things business and personal: "Is it the truth? Is it fair to all concerned? Will it build goodwill and better friendships? Will it be beneficial to all concerned?"

The Golden Rule shows up in the code of ethics of the National Society of Fund Raising Executives. Among other things, the code declares that members "recognize their stewardship responsibility to ensure that needed resources are vigorously and ethically sought and that the intent of the donor is honestly fulfilled." It further states members shall avoid even the appearance of misconduct in their fund-raising activities. See Appendix II for the full code and Appendix III for a Donor Bill of Rights.

Simple is Not Always Easy

In his 1896 novel, *In His Steps,* Charles Monroe Sheldon wrote of a local church whose members pledged for one year not to do anything without asking, "What would Jesus Do?" Here is what the book's main character, Pastor Henry Maxwell, told his church one Sunday morning:

"I want volunteers from the First Church who will pledge themselves, earnestly and honestly for an entire year, not to do anything without first asking the question, 'What would Jesus do?' And after asking that question, each one will follow Jesus as exactly as he knows how, no matter what the result may be. I will of course include myself in this company of volunteers, and shall take for granted that my church here will not be surprised at my future conduct, as based upon this standard of action, and will not oppose whatever is done if they think Christ would do it."[3]

As you can imagine, the results of the challenge were as varied as the individual interpretations of what Jesus would do. Families became estranged, relationships were fractured, and jobs were lost. Some church members never recovered from their sufferings and others became stronger in their faith and more energized in their testimonies.

No one knows exactly when, but What Would Jesus Do became WWJD and WWJD became a movement. Sheldon's great-grandson, Garrett W. Sheldon, retold the 1896 story in a contemporary setting in his 1993 book, *What Would Jesus Do?* Today, companies produce WWJD bracelets and other jewelry, CDs, coffee mugs, and clothing. Coverage of WWJD activities has been on television and radio and in magazines and newspapers. Dozens of websites offer products, services, and testimonies of WWJD life-changing experiences.

It is an Individual and an Organizational Commitment

Ethical behavior at its simplest is doing the right thing — being honest, decent, humane, and fair. Doing the right thing touches many lives and not everyone agrees on which action is the right thing. That is the hard part in doing the Lord's work — doing the *Lord's* work, moving forward His agenda, not ours. Not only must the donor and the fund raiser be ethical, the recipient church must operate in an environment in which anything less than the highest ethical behavior is not tolerated.

Independent Sector, a national leadership forum for non-profits, corporations, and foundations, states: "The basic means by which we can ensure confidence in philanthropic

Table 6.1 The Aspen Declaration[5]

1. The next generation will be the stewards of our communities, nation, and planet in extraordinarily critical times.

2. The present and future well-being of our society requires an involved, caring citizenry with good moral character.

3. People do not automatically develop good moral character; therefore, conscientious efforts must be made to help young people develop the values and abilities necessary for moral decision making and conduct.

4. Effective character education is based on core ethical values which form the foundation of democratic society, in particular, respect, responsibility, trustworthiness, caring, justice and fairness, and civic virtue and citizenship.

5. These core ethical values transcend cultural, religious, and socio-economic differences.

6. Character education is, first and foremost, an obligation of families; it is also an important obligation of faith communities, schools, youth, and other human-service organizations.

7. These obligations to develop character are best achieved when these groups work in concert.

8. The character and conduct of our youth reflect the character and conduct of society; therefore, every adult has the responsibility to teach and model the core ethical values and every social institution has the responsibility to promote the development of good character.

---

and voluntary organizations is to demonstrate the quality of our leadership. This demonstration begins with full and consistent evidences that trustees, staff, directors and all other participants reflect habitually the ethics people have a right to expect of them and that they make ethical practices part of the organization's culture."[4]

The Josephson Institute of Ethics declares that there are six pillars of character upon which we should make ethical choices: trustworthiness, respect, responsibility, fairness, caring, and citizenship. An Institute-sponsored group of educators, ethicists, and youth-service professionals met in Aspen, Colorado, in 1992 and folded the six-pillars concept into what they call The Aspen Declaration, shown in Table 6.1.

It is a reality of human relationships that people cannot be compelled to behave ethically. Your church can enlist the best volunteers and hire the best staff, give them the best training and the best mentoring, and provide the best worship experiences and the best spiritual support. When push comes to shove, though, ethical behavior is an individual decision. "The heart is deceitful above all things, and desperately wicked: who can know it?" (Jeremiah 17:9) That makes the field of personnel development an inexact science, as Richard Bergstrom discovered. A few months after he became pastor at a Colorado church his youth pastor confessed to eight years of embezzling church funds.[6]

"The only way to protect oneself and others is not to provide the opportunity in the first place," Bergstrom says. "The fatal mistake of many pastors and churches is to assume they and those around them are above such temptations."[7] After the embezzling incident Pastor Bergstrom put into place financial and personnel policies to protect the church and individuals from temptation and from accusation. His recommendations are shown in Table 6.2.

Put it in Writing

Scandals among nonprofits in the past ten years have caused many organizations to examine their ethical practices. Non-profit associations in several states are developing standards to promote ethical behavior and accountability

Table 6.2 Guidelines for Handling Church Funds[8]

Persons who handle church funds should
1. Have made a generous pledge to the church.

2. Be up-to-date on all pledge payments.

3. Have no hint of reputation as a free spender.

4. Have a good reputation in the community.

It is good business to
1. Count and record offerings immediately after they are received.

2. Store offerings in a secure or well-supervised area.

3. Count cash and checks twice for accuracy.

4. Place offerings in lockbags provided by the bank.

5. Place the lockbags in a safe or night depository until the bank opens.

6. Strictly limit who has access to the safe.

7. Change the safe combination when someone is no longer authorized to use it.

8. Make sure the same person is not involved in more than one of the financial procedures of the church.

9. Persons authorized to write checks against church funds are held responsible through an accounting/auditing system.

10. Provide the bank with annual updates of persons authorized to sign checks against any account associated with the church.

11. Issue annual receipts for giving.

Effective policies include
1. Membership in the Evangelical Council for Financial Accountability.

2. Not allowing pre-signed checks.

3. Documentation of all expenses.

4. Not paying expenses out of cash offerings.

5. Not writing checks for cash amounts.

6. Not mingling funds.

7. Not having separate accounts in the church's name.

8. Authorization for use of funds for special purposes.

---

among their members and to strengthen the public trust.[9] For Christian nonprofits, the Evangelical Council for Financial Accountability assists its members in maintaining the highest ethical standards.

If your church is seriously involved in fund raising you should have gift acceptance guidelines that go beyond the everyday processes of handling offerings. When properly written and adhered to, the guidelines relieve you and other church leaders of making decisions regarding common and challenging gift situations.

The guidelines should be written by a church committee made up of the pastor, at least one board member, several members who are knowledgeable regarding fund raising, and several members who are knowledgeable regarding financial management. Check with your local or nearest chapter of the National Society of Fund Raising Executives for nonprofits which may have guidelines to which you could refer.

The Board Reviews A Draft

A draft of your guidelines should be given to the board for its review and tentative approval. The board will want to be assured the contents are moving in the right direction. The guidelines are then given to all members for their review and suggested improvements. In a very large church this could be done through discussion groups of staffs and volunteers at the departmental level. After all members have had opportunity for input, the guidelines go back to the board for appropriate changes and final approval. We say appropriate changes because the board may not wish to make all of the changes suggested by members. Changes suggested by members should not be rejected out of hand, however, since the board would want members to know it is responsive to their concerns.

Use A Three-Ring Binder

Keep the approved guidelines in a three-ring binder so they can be revised from time to time. Minor revisions can be made by the board. You may want to bring major revisions before the church. Make spiral-bound copies or stapled copies of the approved guidelines available to all fund-raising staff and volunteers and to members who request them.

Listed below are the basic elements of gift acceptance guidelines for church fund-raising. Format and appearance can be what works best for your church. You will want to add enough narrative to explain clearly the criteria for the managing and accounting methods you plan to use. Some of the elements are similar to those which could be included in separate guidelines for regular church offerings and gifts.

Do not get hung up on the use of the words *program* and *campaign*. They are often used interchangeably and that is okay, but there are differences. Campaigns are conducted to secure funding for programs. A campaign has a starting and ending time. This assures participants of an accounting period and signals when gifted funds likely will be expended. Program usually refers to on-going activities which may or may not be related to fund raising. It is quite acceptable, though, to speak of fund-raising programs.

Gift Acceptance Guidelines

I. Forms of Gifts. What forms of gifts will the church accept? How will gifts be processed and who will process them?
   A. Checks
   B. Cash
   C. Payroll deductions
   D. Bank drafts
   E. Credit cards
   F. Debit Cards
   G. Electronic transfers

II. Types of Gifts. What types of gifts will be accepted? How will they be valued? Who is authorized to accept them?
   A. Public stocks
   B. Closely-held stocks
   C. Bonds
   D. Mutual funds
   E. Real estate
   F. Personal property
   G. Gifts-in-kind
   H. Insurance policies
   I. Bequests
   J. Trusts, revocable and irrevocable
   K. Annuities
   L. Out-of-pocket expenses
   M. Pooled income funds
   N. Residence with life-time use reserved

Note: The tax treatment of these types of gifts is a matter of law. Your policies could state that you do not accept some of them or any of them. If you wish to accept them, consult your attorney on writing this part. In the case of real estate gifts, be sure you have inspected the property, the title work is clean and donor conditions do not violate your policies. Your attorney can advise you on the requirements of such things as environmental assessment, building inspection, and property with indebtedness.

III. Sources of Gifts. What are the sources of gifts?
  A. Church members
  B. Former church members who have moved away
  C. Non-members who have an interest in your church programs
  D. Corporations, including vendors
  E. Foundations
  F. Fund-raising events
  G. Other churches
  H. Non-profit organizations

Note: Descriptions of methods to identify, cultivate and solicit persons within the groups could be included in the guidelines or they could be a separate report.

IV. Uses of Gifts. How will donors be assured their gifts will be used for purposes they requested? For what purposes will gifts be used and who decides the uses?
  A. Unrestricted
  B. Restricted
  C. Programs and missions
  D. Capital expenditures
  E. Current operations
  F. Endowments for specified purposes
  G. Donor designated
  H. Board designated
V. Acknowledgments and Receipts.
  A. How will gifts be acknowledged and by whom?
  B. Will receipts also be issued?
  C. Acknowledgments and thank-you letters should be mailed within three working days of receiving the gift.
  D. Acknowledgments may be accompanied by receipts.

Note: Acknowledgments should be in the form of individually addressed and personally signed letters. This is an opportunity for the pastor, campaign leader, or volunteer to say thank you. Acknowledgments should not be impersonal pre-printed forms. The IRS requires that a written acknowledgment be sent to donors for gifts of $250 or more. For gifts of all sizes the IRS requires that donors be told whether any goods or services were provided in return for the gift. It is good practice to include the goods-and-services statement with each acknowledgment, although some churches do it once yearly.

VI.   Donor Recognition. How will donors be recognized and at what levels of gifts?
    A. Naming opportunities
    B. Individual plaques, certificates
    C. Display names on an Honor Wall of Donors or similar
    D. Publish names in a Sunday bulletin or a recognition booklet
    E. Pulpit announcements
    F. Recognition luncheon or dinner
    G. List donors in an annual report
    H. Anonymous at the donor's request

Note: Donors should be recognized for the amount they paid not the amount they pledged. The IRS does not recognize gifts of personal or professional services as charitable contributions. That does not prevent your church from showing appreciation to donors of services in some of the ways mentioned above, or in other ways which may be appropriate for the situation.

VII. Types of Programs. What types of fund-raising programs will be undertaken: annual, capital, endowment?
    A. Will pledges be accepted? If so, over what period may they be paid: one year, three years, five

years? Will pledgers be sent reminders monthly, quarterly, semi-annually, annually?

B. Gifts and pledges received prior to the start of gift counting for a campaign should not be counted toward the goal. Earnings on invested funds should not be counted toward the goal at any time. You may count estate commitments established before the start of a campaign when they are made known for the first time during the campaign.

C. Write job descriptions for key persons and groups. Construct an organizational chart of committees and staff members for staff and volunteers. Rather than using a chart, you could include a statement of lines of responsibilities. An option is to include this information in a separate report.

D. When will progress/accountability reports be presented to church members: annually, semi-annually, quarterly, monthly? Who will prepare the reports and what information will be included?

Note: The Financial Accounting Standards Board (FASB) has standards for reportable revenues for churches and other nonprofits. You should discuss these with your accountant. In tracking progress toward a campaign goal it is good practice to count gifts only when they are received and to count pledges only when they are in writing.

VIII. Information Privacy. What methods will be in place to assure privacy?

A. Who in the church has authorized access to the information?

B. Under what circumstances will information be released to law enforcement or other governmental agencies?

C. Who is designated to release information?

Note: All biographical and fund information of prospects and donors is strictly confidential, to be used for church purposes only. This includes privileged information that is written or spoken. The names of donors and members should not be sold to or shared with other organizations, nonprofit or for profit.

IX.   Investments. Who is in charge of investing funds?
    A. Will a church committee be responsible for managing investments or will an investment manager be hired?
    B. Will the investment manager be an individual or a firm?
    C. Who will be the church's representative in dealing with the manager?
    D. Will you allow church members affiliated with investment firms to bid for your investment business in behalf of their firms?
    E. If you plan to invest only in companies with socially or morally responsible products or services are you prepared to receive lower rates of return?
    F. What ratio of funds, within a range, will be in stocks, bonds, and certificates of deposit?
    G. What ratio of funds, within a range, will be in long-term investments, short-term investments, or cash accounts?
    H. What investment purchases will be declared as unacceptable?
    I. What reporting and accountability measures will be in place?

Note: The area of investments can be technical, complex, and volatile. In establishing your investment guidelines you should seek help from an experienced stock broker or investment counselor. To avoid a conflict of interest, select someone who is not affiliated with your church.

X. Conflict of Interest. What constitutes a conflict of interest?
   A. Which persons will be required to disclose conflicts of interest?
   B. How will disclosure be made and to whom?
   C. If a member discloses conflict of interest will the member then be allowed to vote or otherwise participate in the matter involving the disclosure?
   D. Will an undisclosed conflict of interest cause an official action to be taken against those involved?

Note: Rather than allowing disclosures you may wish to make conflicts of interest unacceptable in the first place.

CHECKLIST FOR SUCCESS

Date Completed

_____ Think of a time when you had to choose whether to accept a gift of questionable nature or with unreasonable restrictions. Was your response an easy or hard decision? Would you do anything differently next time?

_____ With several other persons, review *this week* your congregation's systems for counting and depositing funds. Revise as needed. A good plan protects honest people from accusations.

_____ Utilizing leadership at the board level, begin drafting gift acceptance guidelines, even if you are not in a special campaign at this time. If you have gift acceptance guidelines review them periodically to be sure they are in line with current laws and that they meet the current needs of your congregation.

_____ Keep a diary of the difficult ethical situations you encounter during the next year. Note how you handle them. What are the strengths and weaknesses of what you did? What steps could have been taken to prevent them from occurring? From getting out of control? Without sharing confidential information on individual cases, ask several respected members who are experienced or trained in such matters to recommend preventative measures as guidelines for your congregation. This may require board involvement and approval. A local college professor in this field could provide direction. Revisit the measures regularly and make adjustments as needed.

_____ Make a file of newspaper and magazine articles and advertisements with questionable ethical situations. Is everything clear cut? What would you do in the situations? What could you do to change the situations you read about or see? Is trying to change them worth your trouble?

CELEBRATE SUCCESS

List the most valuable ideas you received from this chapter. Set target dates and name persons responsible for implementation, including yourself. List ways to articulate to members and friends of the church the intended or anticipated benefits of the ideas. Create ways to celebrate the successful achievement of the benefits.

NOTES

1   Richard L. Bergstrom, Gary Fenton, Wayne A. Pohl, *Mastering Church Finance*, 121. © 1992 by Christianity Today, Inc. Reprinted by permission of Multnomah Publishers, Inc.

2   Michael O'Neill, "A Spare Literature," *Advancing Philanthropy*, Summer 1997: 26-30.

3   Charles Monroe Sheldon, *In His Steps* (New York: Books, Inc., 1960), 15.

4   Independent Sector, *Ethics and the Nation's Voluntary and Philanthropic Community* (Washington, D.C.: Independent Sector, 1991), 9, 10.

5   The Aspen Declaration is derived from Character Counts!, a project of the Josephson Institute of Ethics, Marina del Rey, California. Used by permission.

6   Bergstrom, 115. Used by permission.

7   Bergstrom, 117. Used by permission.

8   Bergstrom, 119-123. Used by permission.

9   Stephen G. Greene, "State Associations Draft Ethical Standards to Bolster Trust in Charities," *The Chronicle of Philanthropy*, July 16, 1998: 44.

7
Affirmations of Stewardship — Why We Raise Money

Here we are at the end, and I'm pretty well worn out. You've covered a lot of information, and I must say that I haven't agreed with all of it."

We understand how that would be a natural reaction. Our hope is that what we have presented will get you started on a program of meaningful fund raising and help you stay with it. Your success is our success.

"The difficulty for me is trying to bring into my church environment the fund-raising practices I have perceived over the years as being too secular for me to consider. Yet, I know I need to do more than I'm doing if our church ministries are going to be sufficiently funded for maintenance and growth."

We began by saying change is often uncomfortable and that most pastors and other church leaders are not trained in fund-raising principles and practices. Although what we have presented does not constitute all of the training you should have, our purpose was twofold: to take the mystery out of fund raising and to challenge you to consider new concepts. You are well on your way to fund-raising success.

We wish you the best of everything good and great for your church.

"But, you have a little more to share."

Yes, we want to give you some final perspectives on the relationship of biblical stewardship principles to real-world situations, to help you understand why we raise money.

"I'm here to learn."

Cecil B. DeMille and Stewardship

Cecil B. DeMille was a director, producer, editor, actor, and writer whose credits include more than 100 movies and plays.[1] His work spanned the eras of silent and sound films. He was known for his obsession for realism — he once used real bullets in a scene — and for his splashy and expensive films, including *King of Kings*, *Samson and Delilah*, and *The Ten Commandments*. He produced *The Ten Commandments* in 1923 and again in 1956. It was a big success both times.[2]

"Give me any page in the Bible and I will give you a movie," he is supposed to have said. Although this statement is of dubious authenticity, it is characteristic of his audacity and authoritative style.

We contend that on any page in the Bible there is a story of stewardship. The biblical principles of stewardship and modern principles of fund raising can be united into a powerful force, a force to renew your church and return the joy of giving to the lives of donor/stewards.

God is the creator and owner of all that is in existence. We are co-creators with God and stewards of His creations. (Genesis, Chapters 1, 2, 3) Thus, we have a responsibility that goes beyond preserving our produce or being merely consumers of the produce of others. We must strive to increase what we have and be prepared to account for it, as Jesus declared in the parable of the talents. (Matthew 25:14-30)

We have said fund-raising techniques enable people to give. They are not substitutes for committed hearts. Even though techniques can help people do the right thing, techniques will not change attitudes about giving. Nothing we, nor you, can do will motivate people to give unless they want to give. The decision is totally up to them. The priorities they place on their personal values will drive their giving. How they view their response to God's love in relationship to family, career, recreation, and dozens of other things that impact their lives will determine the extent of their support of church ministries. "Your heart will be in the same place as your treasure." (Matthew 6:21)

Stewardship is far more than responding to an annual tithing sermon or annual membership fund drive. It is a way of life that celebrates God as the creator who has placed this wonderful world in our hands and asked us to care for it and live with it in harmony and make it better.

"Christian stewardship," wrote church administrator William J. Keech, "is the dedication of all I am and have, under the control of God's Spirit in Christ, to the doing of his will, in recognition of his lordship, in gratitude for his love, in every area of my life, and in the service of his redemptive fellowship."[3]

The Bible teaches stewardship around four major themes: environment, money, giftedness, and service.[4] Many scriptures on the themes help us understand ways we can effectively respond to God's call for stewardship in our lives. Following are some responses we hope are helpful in your search for understanding.

Affirming the Stewardship of Environment

The choices of topics on environmental stewardship are many and varied. We could cover issues relating to Yellowstone National Park, the first area in the world to be designated a national park; the Dust Bowl years of the 1930's, which were a wake-up call to action on conservation; or the public and private partnerships trying to save the Florida Everglades. As well, you could easily identify issues relating to the quality of air, water, waste, toxic chemicals, and pesticides in your town and neighborhood.

There is also an environmental issue in neighborhoods that, too often, get little attention — the church building and grounds. Is the physical appearance of your church property inviting? There is no way of knowing how often potential worshipers choose to drive past rather than drive in, because of a non-inviting appearance. Are there physical deficiencies inside your building which may keep visitors from returning? Again, there is no way of knowing how often this occurs, only that it is possible.

We are not saying that physical appearance is the lone factor that individuals and families use to decide where to worship. We are saying it can influence their decision. Determine how the following Church Environmental analysis applies to your property and act accordingly. Your denomination may have specific guidelines.

Church Environmental Analysis

1. Off-Property View

a. The church can be seen easily from the road.
b. The church sign is readable, lighted, and well painted.
c. The yard and grounds are mowed, trimmed, and well maintained.
d. The building looks well maintained.

2. Building Exterior

a. A safe entrance/exit to the parking area is provided.
b. The parking lot is surfaced, neatly lined, and appropriately lighted, and concrete bumpers are used.

There is available space closest to the building for visitors and those with special needs.

c. Sidewalks have even surfaces and are edged, free of clutter and trash, and landscaped appropriately for the time of year.

d. Signs indicate the location of the sanctuary and office.

e. Entrance to the building is equipped for those with special needs.

f. The building is in good repair and does not need painting. Entrance/exits are clean, including eaves, porches, welcome mats.

g. Windows are clean, consistent with the appearance from the outside. Patio areas are landscaped, furnished, clean, comfortable, and inviting.

3. Entry Foyer

a. Entrance is through a glass door.

b. Environment is inviting, decorated in good taste; marketing materials are attractively and conveniently displayed.

c. Greeters are present who assist visitors with name tags.

d. Signs clearly and visibly direct persons unfamiliar with the building's floor plan.

4. Building Interior

a. Rest rooms are clean, well maintained, and without leaky faucets. Rooms are tastefully decorated and not isolated so that children's safety is assured.

b. Exit signs are fully functional. Exits are accessible for those with special needs.

c. Ceilings are well maintained and free of damage from water leaks and water stains.

d. Walls, handrails, doors, and door facings are in good repair and clean.

e. Floors are clean and well maintained, with no conditions to cause concern that insects are present.

f. Offices are professional in appearance, business-like, well furnished, organized, and tastefully decorated.

g. Offices, classrooms, and restrooms are clearly identified with appropriate signs and numbers and are handicapped accessible.

5. Sanctuary

a. Well lighted, temperature controlled. Seating is comfortable, view of the rostrum is unobstructed, wheel chair locations are available, and sound system meets needs of hearing impaired persons.

b. Hymnals, Bibles, and brochures are available and in good condition.

c. Regular attendees sit in the middle of the rows toward the front, leaving space for visitors near the aisles and toward the rear of the sanctuary.

6. Religious Education Department

a. Bulletin boards are visible for all ages, well maintained, and with current information.

b. Classrooms are clean and well maintained, with storage available for supplies. Tables and chairs are appropriate sizes for the age of students.

c. Personnel files are kept on children's teachers and workers, containing background information to guard against pedophiles.

d. Infection control measures are utilized regularly in cleaning toys and equipment.

e. Smoke alarms and fire extinguishers are accessible, exit doors are clearly marked and easily accessible, a fire/disaster plan is posted, and staff are trained in implementing the plan.

7. Kitchen / Fellowship Hall*

a. Hand washing facilities are available, hand washing procedures are posted, and the procedures are routinely followed by each person working in the kitchen. Disposable gloves are provided and used by persons handling and serving food.

b. Cleaning chemicals are kept in original containers and stored separately from food items and out of reach of small children. Insecticides and other poisons are not stored in the kitchen.

c. Potable water (safe for drinking) is provided from a source constructed to preclude back flow. The water source and delivery are operated according to state health regulations.

d. Refrigerator contains a thermometer and maintains a temperature of no more than 45 degrees. Cold foods should be served at temperatures of at least 45 degrees, hot foods should be served at temperatures of at least 140 degrees.

e. For manual dish washing, there is a three-compartment sink for washing, rinsing, and sanitizing. Sponges are not used for dish washing.

*These are minimum suggestions. Obtain and follow your state health department requirements and guidelines for food handling and sanitation procedures.

Affirming the Stewardship of Money

The Bible speaks clearly, meaningfully, and extensively regarding money.

"Jesus talked about money in 16 of the recorded 38 New Testament parables," says pastor Brian Bauknight. "Jesus spoke five times as often about money and earthly possessions as he did about prayer. A careful researcher can find 500 verses in the Bible on prayer and a few more than 500 on faith. But more than 2,000 verses in the Bible are concerned with money and possessions."[5] Only the Kingdom of God is mentioned more often than money.

As noted by Roy W. Menninger in Chapter Two, contributors are motivated by varying degrees of altruism and selfishness, and these motives often impact at the same time. We may generalize that the amounts and purposes of giving are as varied as people are different. On a continuum of giving the range seems mind boggling: from the poor widow who put her last two pennies into the Temple collection box (Mark 12:41–44), to communications mogul Ted Turner who pledged one-billion dollars to the United Nations in 1997.

Looking across the continuum we would also come to the name Ethel Hawkins, of Pine Bluff, Arkansas. Born in 1911, Ethel is a retired teacher and the widow of a Presbyterian pastor. She has a modest income, does not live extravagantly, and does not own a car. Yet, during her lifetime she has contributed more than $300,000 to churches, higher education, and farmers in third-world countries. Organizations which have benefited from her extraordinary generosity include the Heifer Project International, churches in rural North Carolina and Arkansas, Barber-Scotia College, Johnson C. Smith University (from which she graduated in 1936), high schools in Puerto Rico and Haiti, the Southern Poverty Law Center, the NAACP, and the Presbyterian Church (U.S.A.) Foundation.

In 1991 she was named the Outstanding Philanthropist of the Year by the National Society of Fund Raising Executives. In her acceptance speech in San Antonio, she gave the Lord all the credit for her philanthropy. After the ceremony, people flocked to the stage to congratulate her. One person kissed her and said, "When I grow up I want to be just like you."

Ethel has been featured in *Horizons*, a publication for Presbyterian women, and honored by the National Black Presbyterian Caucus.[6]

Affirming the Stewardship of Giftedness

The Holy Spirit works with us in many different ways to accomplish God's purposes. (I Corinthians 12:4-30) Some people can sing beautifully. Others can write and speak well. Some have the gift of studying, or teaching, or the gift of faith for testifying to others. Still others have gifts to cure illnesses, care for family members and friends, build superhighways, invent labor-saving machines, speak for the disenfranchised, grow vegetables and flowers, dream us to the moon, manage businesses, lead nations, or make peace.

A Change of Attitude

When David L. Heetland was a pastor he was deeply satisfied by helping people find meaning in their lives. He initially regarded fund raising as a necessary imposition to meet the church budget, a diversion from the real ministry of preaching, pastoral care, and teaching. He left the pastorate to become a campus minister and teacher of religion at a church-related university, a move that strengthened the conviction of his calling. When the university president asked him to be director of fund raising he reluctantly accepted, unsure what satisfactions fund raising would bring. He soon discovered the many joys of partnerships with persons interested in making a positive difference through their financial gifts. Today, as a fund development officer at a seminary, he continues to help people fulfill the best in themselves.[7]

"The fact is that I have come to see fund raising not simply as a satisfying career but as a vitally important ministry," says Heetland. "This ministry provides adequate financial undergirding for critically important work. Some suggest that lack of funding is the major impediment to eradicating hunger, developing self-help programs, and spreading the gospel of Jesus Christ. What could be more rewarding than

to enable ministries of relief, development, and proclama-
tion to be carried out in Christ's name?"[8]

Limitations Can be Blessings

In another setting, a pastor was struggling with a new
assignment and asked his long-time friend, Dorsey Levell, to
do a revival series. "I turned him down, because I don't have
the gift of being an evangelist," Levell recalls. "God has
made it very clear to me that my strongest gift is in the area
of administration, especially fund-raising administration."
The pastor pressed his case and out of their conversations
came the idea for a stewardship revival.

They planned four sessions accompanied by simple
meals, beginning on Sunday. "The selection of low-fat,
highly nutritious food each evening demonstrated stewardship of our bodies," says Levell. His first sermon was on
basic stewardship, using Matthew 25 as the foundation. He
presented a broad concept of stewardship and previewed
the three services to follow.

The Sunday evening theme was stewardship of time.
Levell covered the importance of making the most of the 24
hours given to every person, rich or poor, professional or
laborer, homemaker or wage earner. Time management
was presented as responsible stewardship, including setting
priorities for family, business and church. Monday evening's
theme was stewardship of abilities and emphasized volunteering for church and community.

Levell thought attendance would drop off dramatically
on Tuesday evening because the topic was money. However,
more people attended that service than any of the other
evenings. Levell spoke of establishing individual goals for
giving, reasons for giving, and the value of having a personal giving plan. He said when church programs meet the
needs of members they will give more to the church.

"Being a donor/steward means decisions must be made
for ourselves, our family, our church, and our world," Levell

said. "We can't give to everything, so we must make choices and establish priorities. Your choices will be different than mine. By making a plan for giving we maximize our joy of giving and reduce the guilt of saying no to many good causes. Our plans should be reviewed periodically for any adjustments we might want to make."

Affirming the Stewardship of Service

Donors and prospective donors want to see value for their gift dollars. They want to be assured their gift investments have a return which satisfies their needs. Churches with successfully funded ministries demonstrate they are meeting those needs by the quality of their leadership. Key leadership attributes are shown in Table 7.1.

Leadership of this high caliber is exemplified by the Sisters of the Presentation of the Blessed Virgin Mary. Their motto is "Doing What Needs to be Done." The order was founded in 1775 in Cork, Ireland, by Nano Nagle. Their motto is based on a statement in the Nagle family coat of arms, *Non vos sed votum,* which is usually translated as "Not Words but Deeds."

Nano Nagle came from a wealthy family and was educated in France at a time when England's governance of Ireland prohibited formal education of Catholics. She illegally started schools for boys and girls in County Cork, at first behind hedges — called hedge schools — and later in attics and spare rooms of sympathizers. In an era when nuns were required by law to carry out their activities within convent walls, she walked the streets providing comfort, medicine, and clothing to the needy, using up her inheritance.[10]

Today the order is small, with approximately 3,200 Sisters in seventeen countries.

How One Congregation Does It

A congregation of the order in Fargo, North Dakota, owns and operates a retirement home, two hospitals, and the state's largest program for persons who are developmentally disabled. The Sisters call these their sponsored ministries. At their convent, they maintain an infirmary to provide emergency care to Sisters and permanent care of Sisters who become unable to care for themselves because of illness or age.

Each of the congregation's sponsored ministries is an independent nonprofit corporation with its own CEO and staff, including a staff member in charge of fund raising. The fund raisers are also responsible for volunteer programs and community outreach. There is an umbrella foundation to oversee all fund raising activities. The CEO's of the sponsored ministries are members of the foundation board of directors, as are key community leaders. The foundation office is in the convent and is staffed by a full-time paid secretary.

The Focus is on Mission

"We are organized in ways which enable us to give better service," Sister Paula Ringuette, president of the congregation and the foundation, told the authors. "Our service is not just something we do. It is who we are. Our mission is to live out our baptismal commitment according to gospel values."

The congregation undertook a $3 million fund-raising campaign in 1995. The money came from friends, corporations, constituents and their families, and staff members. It was used to develop and expand the Sisters' counseling and support services, construct a new clinic building and much-needed renovations at the older of the two hospitals, and strengthen their endowment fund for retirement needs. Fund-raising counsel directed the sixteen-month campaign.

Table 7.1 Leadership Donors Expect[9]

Vision

To encourage people to give generously, the leaders of the congregation must provide the church with a detailed and realistic picture of a preferable future.

Integrity

Congregants need visual and experiential assurance that the people overseeing the financial matters of the church are beyond reproach.

Credibility

An effective leader must describe realistic ministry plans, offer plausible information and situational analyses, and come with a proven track record of promises and subsequent performance.

Competence

The leaders of the church will serve as the stewards for the stewards; therefore, the prospective donor typically strives to determine how competent the leaders of the church have been in fulfilling their past responsibilities.

Enthusiasm

Donors need to believe they are giving to something that is more significant than survival, more exciting than just a job, more influential than institutional religious practice.

Courage

When a leader steps out in faith, confidently proclaiming God's promises for the church, boldly challenging the people of God and aggressively taking the point on the march into the unknown, people are more likely to follow.

Impact

People want their giving to count; they measure the "profitability" of their giving by how much of a difference their benevolence made in the lives of people.

A Tale of Two Churches

There are many reasons why some congregations grow and fulfill their purpose and others remain stagnant or die. In general, the differences between living and dying congregations are in the ways members look at possibilities, as shown in Table 7.2.

Church consultant Kennon L. Callahan says there is a common thread among them. It is not fund raising. It is not philanthropy. It is not stewardship. It is not giving. It is not management, or marketing, or leadership. It is not any of the definitional nuances of these terms. It is mission. Mission-driven congregations, he says, never have enough money because they give it away in support of their mission. Congregations that are not mission-driven never have enough money because they have forgotten their mission.

"People do not give generously to congregations that have allowed mission to recede into the background," he says. "When the focus of meeting after meeting is primarily on getting enough money to balance the budget, people's generous impulses wither."[12]

Similarly, the founder of Saddleback Valley Community Church in Orange County, California, Rick Warren, says "that growing, healthy churches have a clear-cut identity. They understand their reason for being; they are precise in their purpose. They know exactly what God has called them to do."[13]

This Church Decided to Quit

Downtown's Faith United Church was started in 1840 by the town's founders. At one time, it was one of the largest and best managed of its denomination in the state, a model others looked to for its strength, its faith, and its impact in the community. Over the years, the downtown

Table 7.2 Differences Between Living and Dying Congregations[11]

Living Congregations:

- Are proactive and focus on their positive vision for the future.

- Build on and are renewed by their vision.

- Engage in mission through witness and seize opportunities to meet needs.

- Focus outward and share in ministry with others.

Dying Congregations:

- Are reactive to problems and surrender control.

- Doubt their control over the future.

- Doubt their positive vision of the future.

- Have lost their zeal for ministy and miss opportunities to minister.

- Focus inward and become the recipients of ministry.

---

area slipped into urban decay, as people and businesses moved to the suburbs. The church's programs began to focus more on older members, at a time when young families preferred churches with strong youth programs. Identification and cultivation of prospective new members came to a standstill, as did the spiritual growth of the church. Membership went from a high of 1,500 in 1970 to 700 in 1997; Sunday attendance fell to less than 25% of membership.

The regional administration assigned a pastor to do a turnaround. The enthusiastic new pastor talked of expanding ministries to include a daycare center, a youth program, community outreach, and other activities to meet the new needs of the downtown area. These things would require more staff, more volunteers, additional parking, and additional funds.

A heated controversy developed. Many members resisted the proposed changes. Some moved their memberships to other congregations. Others quit attending. Those who stayed did not participate. They did not want to change with the times, nor plan for the future. They wanted to remember the past. One member stated in a discussion session, "We want things to be the way they were until we die."

Faith United Church became a church without a mission. Discipleship and evangelism deteriorated because members acted on their own agenda, not God's. A continually shrinking membership was unwilling to respond to the love of God and unable to partake of the blessings He would have them receive.

This Church Decided to Change

North Hill Church was located just outside the city limits near a landfill. Attendance peaked at approximately 100 persons in the 1960s. It shrank steadily after that because of decreasing property values and other economic problems. There was a vote in 1989 on whether to close the church. Members decided to struggle on, believing that God was not through with them. In 1990, there were twenty-two people present to welcome a new pastor and his wife.

"I dare you to out-give God," the young pastor challenged his members. They started a building fund, with a goal of $15,000, to repair the roof and to replace windows and doors. Shortly after the new windows and doors were installed, the building was destroyed by an arsonist. With donated land from another church, they rebuilt on ten acres away from the landfill, but still in the country.

In 1992, at their new location in a modest, 140-seat sanctuary, the pastor asked members where they wanted to be in five years, and to pray about what God would have them do in the next twelve months. Here is what happened:

They mapped a three-mile circle around the building and distributed information packets and pocket-size New Testaments to all residences. The church reached out to college youth with bus ministries. Preaching, teaching, and testimonies from pew and pulpit enlarged their image of God's love for them, and their roles as obedient servant/ministers. Visitors, baptisms, marriages, and enthusiasm increased dramatically. A fifteen-year building loan of $65,000 was paid in three years. A current fifteen-year loan of $350,000 is expected to be paid in six years.

In 1998, twenty members were being supported by the church in foreign missions and forty members in home missions. The church was in the sixth expansion phase of its physical facilities and was planning a seventh. The sanctuary seated 615 and average Sunday morning attendance was 490. Annual giving approached $400,000, compared with $12,000 in 1990.

What is the secret of their success?

"We are involved in something much bigger than ourselves," the pastor told the authors. "A God-size task, for which the people are willing to pay the price of change, in order to see God at work in their lives and in the lives of those they touch."

The White Rabbit

Near the end of *Alice in Wonderland*, the Knave of Hearts is accused of stealing tarts. At the trial, the White Rabbit is about to read some verses of poetry, purported to be evidence against the Knave. The White Rabbit asks the King, "Where shall I begin, please your Majesty?" The King replies, "Begin at the beginning and go on till you come to the end: then stop."

As we come to the end of our book, we hope for you three things: one, that you have found fund raising is no longer a mystery; two, that you feel freer to explore the many possibilities fund raising can bring; three, that you have a clearer understanding of the role of fund raising as an integral part of your church's ministries.

"Keep your eyes focused on the reason for which we raise money," says George Barna. "To enable people to be in right relationship with God, and to facilitate effective biblical ministry to God's people."[14]

CHECKLIST FOR SUCCESS

Date Completed

_____ Search the Bible for teachings on stewardship of environment, money, giftedness, and service. Use the teachings often in sermons, classes, workshops, offertories, dramas, and other settings.

_____ Watch for persons with testimonies in your congregation and your town on the major stewardship themes of the Bible. Invite them to bring their testimonies before your congregation. Do not limit your search to persons of your faith.

_____ Keep a file of newspaper and magazine articles on the major stewardship themes of the Bible involving people in everyday life. Refer to them in sermons and other worship programs as examples of good things happening in today's world.

_____ Refer to the list of benefits you made after reading Chapter One. Make a new list today. After six months of using our recommendations, assess your progress.

_____ Assemble a group of congregational leaders and other interested persons and conduct a class over several weeks using our book as the text. Keep a notebook of the ideas discussed and ways of implementing them.

CELEBRATE SUCCESS

List the most valuable ideas you received from this chapter. Set target dates and name persons responsible for implementation, including yourself. List ways to articulate to members and friends of the church the intended or anticipated benefits of the ideas. Create ways to celebrate the successful achievement of the benefits.

NOTES

1 "The Internet Movie Database.",http://us.imdb.com/ (24 June 1998).

2 Diane McIntyre, *The Silents Majority*., http://www.mdle.com/classicfilm (June 24, 1998).

3 William J. Keech, *The Life I Owe: Christian Stewardship as a Way of Life* (Valley Forge: Judson Press, 1963), 20.

4 Genesis 1:26-31; Proverbs 3:9, 10; 1 Corinthians 12; and Matthew 25:34-46, among others.

5 Brian Bauknight in *The Abingdon Guide to Funding Ministry, Vol. 1*, Donald W. Joiner, and Norma Wimberly, Editors, (Nashville: Abingdon Press, 1995), 12.

6 Information on Ethel Hawkins provided by the National Society of Fund Raising Executives, Washington, DC; Frankie Reynolds, Perryville, Arkansas; and the Presbyterian Church (U.S.A.).

7 David L. Heetland, *Fundamentals of Fund Raising* (Nashville: Discipleship Resources, 1989), 18, 19.

8 Heetland, 20.

9 George Barna, *How to Increase Giving in Your Church* (Ventura, California: Regal Books, 1997), 143-145. Used by permission.

10 Sister Mary Margaret Mooney, *Doing What Needs to be Done* (Fargo: Sisters of the Presentation, 1997), 7-15.

11 Leonard M. Young and Gary W. Logan, *Making Vision Happen* (Independence, Missouri: Herald Publishing House, 1995), 76. Used by permission.

12 Kennon L. Callahan, *Giving and Stewardship in an Effective Church: A Guide for Every Member* (San Francisco: Harper San Francisco, 1992), 4.

13 Rick Warren, *The Purpose-Driven Church* (Grand Rapids: Zondervan, 1995), 82.

14 Barna, 95.

Appendices

Appendix I

Glossary

These are among the terms used most often from the nearly 1,400 listed in *The NSFRE Fund-Raising Dictionary,* Barbara R. Levy and R. L. Cherry, Editors, Copyright© 1996 John Wiley & Sons, Inc. Reprinted by permission.

A

adjusted gross income, in calculating income tax, the total income minus allowable deductions. Deductions for charitable donations are limited to a percentage of the adjusted gross income. Abbr. AGI.

annual fund, total gifts made on a yearly basis to support (in full or in part) yearly budgets or general operations. Also sustaining fund.

annuity, **1a** a series of equal payments to a person annually or at fixed intervals. **1b** An investment that provides this as income for a specified period, such as the duration of the recipient's life. **1c** The right to receive, or the duty to pay, such a payment.

annuity trust, see *charitable lead trust; charitable remainder trust*.

appraisal, **1** the process, act, or an instance of appraising. **2** an estimate of the value, quality, or worth of something.

appreciated property, securities, real estate, tangible personal property, whose current fair market value is greater than its original tax basis.

B

beneficiary, **1** a person, organization, or institution that receives or is entitled to receive benefits. **2** in law, a person or organization that receives, or is named to receive, property or money from such as a will or insurance policy.

bequest, **1** the act of bequeathing. **2** something bequeathed. Also legacy.

board of trustees, see governing board.

C

capital campaign, an intensive fund-raising effort to meet a specific financial goal within a specified period of time for one or more major projects that are out of the ordinary, such as the construction of a facility, the purchase of equipment, or the acquisition of endowment.

capital gain or loss, the difference between the tax basis of a capital asset and the fair market value. The gain or loss is unrealized until after the sale or other disposition. The gain can be either short term or long term.

case statement, a presentation that sets forth a case.

charitable lead trust, a trust from which a charity receives income for the duration of the trust, after which time the principal is either returned to the donor or distributed to other people. This trust may be an annuity trust, which pays a fixed amount, or a unitrust, which pays a variable amount.

charitable organization, an organization that is eligible to receive charitable donations and is tax-exempt under federal tax law.

charitable remainder trust, an irrevocable trust established to provide payments for the life of one or more people or for a term not to exceed twenty years, with the irrevocable remainder being distributed to one or more qualified charities. This trust may be an annuity trust, which pays a fixed amount, or a unitrust, which pays a variable amount.

chief development officer, the highest-ranking development staff member responsible for a development program. Abbr. CDO. See *development*.

consultant, a person with expertise in a specific field of knowledge who is engaged by a client to provide advice and services.

cultivate, to engage and maintain the interest and involvement of (a donor, prospective donor, or volunteer) with an organization's people, programs, and plans.

D

deduction, an amount that can, according to tax law, be deducted from income or from transfers of assets, thereby reducing tax liability.

deferred gift, a gift (such as a bequest, life insurance policy, charitable remainder trust, gift annuity, or pooled-income fund) that is committed to a charitable organization but is not available for use until some future time, usually the death of the donor. Also gift expectancy.

development, the total process by which an organization increases public understanding of its mission and acquires financial support for its programs.

donor, a person, organization, corporation, or foundation that makes a gift. Also contributor.

donor recognition, the policy and practice of providing recognition to a donor, by a personal letter, a public expression of appreciation, a published list of donors, or in another appropriate way. Also acknowledgment.

E

endowment, a permanently restricted net asset, the principal of which is protected and the income from which may be spent and is controlled by either the donor's restrictions or the organization's governing board.

estate, everything that a person owns.

estate planning, the planned arrangement of a person's assets during his or her lifetime and after death.

estate tax, a federal tax on the net value of an estate before it is divided among heirs.

external affairs, an organization's relations with the public, including its own constituency. Also external relations.

F

fair market value, **1** for the purpose of establishing the value of non-cash gifts, the valuation of property based on what a willing buyer might pay to a willing seller for the property on any given day. **2** the value placed on a benefit or premium received as a result of a donation, ticket, event, etc., a value that is not tax-deductible. Abbr. FMV.

feasibility study, an objective survey, usually conducted by fund-raising counsel, of an organization's fund-raising potential. The study assesses the strength of the organization's case and the availability of its leaders, workers, and prospective donors. The written report includes the study findings, conclusions, and recommendations.

foundation, an organization created from designated funds from which the income is distributed as grants to not-for-profit organizations or, in some cases, to people.

G

gift club, one of various donor categories that are grouped and recognized by a recipient organization on the basis of the level of donations. Also giving club.

gift tax, a tax imposed on the transfer of property as a gift to a non-charitable beneficiary. The tax, imposed upon the donor, is based on the fair market value of the property on the date of the gift.

governing board, people elected or appointed to establish policy, exercise fiscal responsibility, and oversee management. Directors or members of an organization or institution act in accordance with the organization's charter or articles of incorporation (usually reflected in bylaws) to establish policy and oversee management. Also board of directors; board of trustees; governing body.

grant, a financial donation given to support a person, organization, project, or program. Most grants are awarded to not-for-profit organizations.

I

institutional advancement, **1** a process of building awareness and support from all constituent bodies. **2** the programs within an institution that relate to its constituency, including development, public relations, and government relations.

internal relations, the relationships between or among various departments in an organization. Also internal affairs.

Internet, a global computer network consisting of a loose confederation of interconnected networks. The Internet provides many services, such as file transfer, electronic mail, electronic journals and other publications, discussions, and community information service.

L

leadership gift, a gift, donated at the beginning of a campaign, that is expected to set a standard for future giving. Also advance gift.

life interest, an interest or claim that is held only for the duration of the life of the person to whom the interest is given, or for the duration of the life of another person. Also life estate.

living trust, a trust that allows the trustor to keep control of the trust during his or her lifetime by changing its terms and any other conditions. At the trustor's death, a successor trustor can distribute the property to beneficiaries without any court involvement.

living will, a formal document, written by a person while still legally fit and competent to write such a document, stating the wishes of the writer as to how, or if, he or she should be treated medically and supplied with sustenance in the event of a terminal illness.

M

management by objective, an administrative process that sets measurable goals, the achievement of which determines the operation and evaluations of the unit. Abbr. MBO.

marketing, **1a** a process designed to bring about the voluntary exchange of values between a not-for-profit organization and its target market, such as the transfer of a donation in exchange for addressing a social need, recognition, or a feeling of good will. **1b** the process or act of fostering such an exchange in a market.

matching gift, **1** a gift contributed on the condition that it be matched, often within a certain period of time, in accordance with a specified formula. **2** a gift by a corporation matching a gift contributed by one or more of its employees.

media, medium, any means through which something is conveyed (such as television and radio being media of communication) or is accomplished (such as money being a medium of exchange).

mission, an organization's purpose that fulfills a societal need.

N

needs assessment, the study of an organization's program or situation to determine what activity or activities should be initiated or expanded to satisfy a need.

net income unitrust, a type of charitable remainder unitrust that pays to beneficiaries the lesser of a stated percentage of trust assets or the actual net income earned during the year. The trust may contain a make-up provision.

P

payroll deduction, a method by which employees may, upon their written authority, contribute to a campaign by having a specified dollar amount withheld from each pay period.

philanthropy, love of humankind, usually expressed by an effort to enhance the well-being of humanity through personal acts of practical kindness or by financial support of a cause or causes.

phonathon, a telephone campaign to raise money.

planned gift, a gift arranged by gift planning. Also deferred gift; expectancy.

pledge, **1a** a promise that is written, signed, and dated, to fulfill a commitment at some future time; specifically, a financial promise payable according to terms set by the donor. Such pledges may be legally enforceable, subject to state law. **1b** the total amount of such pledge. **2** a verbal pledge.

pooled-income fund, a trust to which a donor transfers property and contributed irrevocably the remainder interest to a qualified charity, retaining a life-income interest for one or more beneficiaries. The transferred property is commingled (pooled) with gifts made by other donors, and each income beneficiary receives a pro rata share of the net income. Upon the death of a beneficiary, the fund's trustee severs from the fund an amount equal to the value upon which the beneficiary's income interest was based and distributes that amount to the charity.

prospect, any potential donor whose linkages, giving ability, and interests have been confirmed.

prospect rating, a procedure for evaluating the giving potential and capacity of a prospect. Also evaluation.

public relations, the activity of developing public awareness among opinion leaders and the general public.

S

solicit, to ask (a person or group) for a contribution of money, resources, a service, or opinion.

T

trustee, **1** a person or institution holding the legal title to property in a trust and having the responsibility for managing it. **2** a member of a governing board.

trustor, a person who creates a trust either by a will or other trust instrument. In the case of a charitable remainder trust, the trustor is a donor.

V

victory celebration, an event, such as a luncheon or dinner, for the leaders of a campaign following its successful completion.

volunteer, to work without compensation in behalf of an organization, cause, benefit, etc. A person who volunteers.

W

will, a legally executed statement of a person's wishes about what is to be done with the person's property after his or her death.

WorldWide Web, an electronic system, connected with the Internet, that allows viewing of images and text and allows sound to be received. Abbr. WWW.

Appendix II

NSFRE Code of Ethical Principles and Standards of Professional Practice

Used by permission of the
National Society of Fund Raising Executives

Statements of Ethical Principles

Adopted November 1991

The National Society of Fund Raising Executives exists to foster the development and growth of fund-raising professionals and the profession, to preserve and enhance philanthropy and volunteerism, and to promote high ethical standards in the fund-raising profession.

To these ends, this Code declares the ethical values and standards of professional practice that NSFRE members embrace and that they strive to uphold in their responsibilities for generating philanthropic support.

Members of the National Society of Fund Raising Executives are motivated by an inner drive to improve the quality of life through the causes they serve. They seek to inspire others through their own sense of dedication and high purpose. They are committed to the improvement of their professional knowledge and skills in order that their performance will better serve others. They recognize their stewardship responsibility to ensure that needed resources are vigorously and ethically sought and that the intent of the donor is honestly fulfilled. Such individuals practice their profession with integrity, honesty, truthfulness and adherence to the absolute obligation to safeguard the public trust.

Furthermore, NSFRE members:

- serve the ideal of philanthropy, are committed to the preservation and enhancement of volunteerism, and hold stewardship of these concepts as the overriding principle of professional life;
- put charitable mission above personal gain, accepting compensation by salary or set fee only;
- foster cultural diversity and pluralistic values, and treat all people with dignity and respect;
- affirm, through personal giving, a commitment to philanthropy and its role in society;
- adhere to the spirit as well as the letter of all applicable laws and regulations;
- bring credit to the fund-raising profession by their public demeanor;
- recognize their individual boundaries of competence and are forthcoming about their professional qualifications and credentials;
- value the privacy, freedom of choice and intersts of all those affected by their actions;
- disclose all relationships that might constitute, or appear to constitute, conflicts of interest;

- actively encourage all their colleagues to embrace and practice these ethical principles; adhere to the following standards of professional practice in their responsibilities for generating philanthropic support.

Standards of Professional Practice

Adopted and incorporated into the NSFRE Code of Ethical Principles November 1992

1. Members shall act according to the highest standards and visions of their institution, profession and conscience.
2. Members shall avoid even the appearance of any criminal offense or professional misconduct.
3. Members shall be responsible for advocating, within their own organizations, adherence to all applicable laws and regulations.
4. Members shall work for a salary or fee, not percentage-based compensation or a commission.
5. Members may accept performance-based compensation, such as bonuses, provided that such bonuses are in accord with prevailing practices within the members' own organizations and are not based on a percentage of philanthropic funds raised.
6. Members shall not pay, seek, or accept finder's fees, commissions or percentage-based compensation for obtaining philanthropic funds and shall, to the best of their ability, discourage their organizations from making such payments.
7. Members shall effectively disclose all conflicts of interest; such disclosure does not preclude or imply ethical impropriety.
8. Members shall accurately state their professional experience, qualifications and expertise.
9. Members shall adhere to the principle that all donor and prospect information created by, or on behalf of, an institution is the property of that institution

and shall not be transferred or utilized except on behalf of that institution.

10. Members shall, on a scheduled basis, give donors the opportunity to have their names removed from lists that are sold to, rented to, or exchanged with other organizations.

11. Members shall not disclose privileged information to unauthorized parties.

12. Members shall keep constituent information confidential.

13. Members shall take care to ensure that all solicitation materials are accurate and correctly reflect the organization's mission and use of solicited funds.

14. Members shall, to the best of their ability, ensure that contributions are used in accordance with donors' intentions.

15. Members shall ensure, to the best of their ability, proper stewardship of charitable contributions, including timely reporting on the use and management of funds and explicit consent by the donor before altering the conditions of a gift.

16. Members shall ensure, to the best of their ability, that donors receive informed and ethical advice about the value and tax implications of potential gifts.

17. Members' actions shall reflect concern for the interests and well-being of individuals affected by those actions. Members shall not exploit any relationship with a donor, prospect, volunteer or employee to the benefit of the member or the member's organization.

18. In stating fund-raising results, members shall use accurate and consistent accounting methods that conform to the appropriate guidelines adopted by the American Institute of Certified Public Accountants (AICPA)* for the type of institution involved. (*In countries outside of the United States, comparable authority should be utilized.)

19. All of the above notwithstanding, members shall
    comply with all applicable local, state, provincial
    and federal civil and criminal laws.

Amended March 1993, October 1994, November 1997

Appendix III

A Donor Bill of Rights

*Developed by: American Association of
Fund-Raising Counsel (AAFRC),
Association for Healthcare Philanthropy (AHP),
Council for Advancement and Support of Education (CASE),
National Society of Fund Raising Executives (NSRE)*

Philanthropy is based on voluntary action for the common good. It is a tradition of giving and sharing that is primary to the quality of life. To assure that philanthropy merits the respect and trust of the general public, and that donors and prospective donors can have full confidence in the not-for-profit organizations and causes they are asked to support, we declare that all donors have these rights:

1. To be informed of the organization's mission, of the way the organization intends to use donated resources, and of its capacity to use donations effectively for their intended purposes.
2. To be informed of the identity of those serving on the organization's governing board, and to expect

the board to exercise prudent judgment in its stewardship responsibilities.

3. To have access to the organization's most recent financial statements.

4. To be assured their gifts will be used for the purposes for which they were given.

5. To receive appropriate acknowledgment and recognition.

6. To be assured that information about their donations is handled with respect and with confidentiality to the extend provided by law.

7. To expect that all relationships with individuals representing organizations of interest to the donor will be professional in nature.

8. To be informed whether those seeking donations are volunteers, employees of the organization or hired solicitors.

9. To have the opportunity for their names to be deleted from mailing lists that an organization may intend to share.

10. To feel free to ask questions when making a donation and to receive prompt, truthful and forthright answers.

Appendix IV

Educational Resources

This is an incomplete list. A complete list would require its own book. The authors intend no endorsement of the listed resources nor non-endorsement of resources not listed.

Although information on services and products is free, resources may charge for their services and products.

Check with your denomination's national headquarters for educational programs and services specific to your faith. Such programs may include workshops, publications, videos, and information on investment vehicles and investment strategies.

Resources	Services
Accountants for the Public Interest 1012 14th Street NW, Suite 906 Washington, DC 20005 Telephone (202) 347–1668 Fax (202) 347–1663	Publishes five booklets for nonprofits: *Classifying 501c Nonprofits, Filing Non-profit Tax Forms, Making Public Disclosures, Selecting Computer Software, Tracking Special Monies.*

American Association of Fund-Raising Counsel and AAFRC Trust for Philanthropy
25 West 43rd Street, Suite 820
New York, NY 10036
Telephone (212) 354–5799
http://www.aafrc.org

Annually publishes *Giving USA* and *Survey of State Laws Regulationg Charitable Solicitations*

Applied Research and Development Institute International
2121 S. Oneida Street, Suite 633
Denver, CO 80222
Telephone (303) 691–6076

Publications and training packages on non-profit management and leadership

Christian Financial Concepts, Inc.
601 Broad Street SE
Gainesville, GA 30501
Telephone (800) 722–1976
Website
http://www.cfcministry.org

Books, workshops and counseling to teach biblical principles of stewardship for individuals and families

Christian Management Association
P. O. Box 4638
Diamond Bar, CA 91765
Telephone (909) 861–8861
Fax (909) 860–8247
E-mail cma@cmaonline.org

Management training and leadership resources

Church Growth Center
1230 U.S. Highway Six
Corunna, IN 46730
Telephone (219) 281–2452
Fax (219) 281–2167
E-mail
churchgrowth@juno.com

Books, materials, consulting for promoting, planning, managing meetings, workshops, and conferences

empty tomb, inc.
301 N. Fourth Street
P. O. Box 2404
Champaign, IL 61825–2404
Telephone (217) 356–9519
Fax (217) 356–2344

Annually publishes *The State of Church Giving*

Evangelical Council
for Financial Accountability
P. O. Box 17456
Washington, DC 20041–0456
Telephone (703) 713–1414
Fax (703) 713–1133
E-mail webmaster@ecfa.org
Website http://www.ecfa.org

Publishes guidelines for ethical practices and financial accountability in churches

The Foundation Center
79 Fifth Avenue
New York, NY 10003–3076
Telephone (212) 620–4230
Website
http://www.fdncenter.org

Publishes directories and guides on corporate and foundation grant makers and proposal writing

The Fund-Raising School
Indiana University Center on
Philanthropy
550 W. North Street, Suite 301
Indianapolis, IN 46202–3162
Telephone (800) 968–6692
E-mail tfrs@iupui.edu
Website http://www.tcop.org

Workshops and publications on fund-raising techniques.

Independent Sector
1828 L Street, NW
Washington, DC 20036
Telephone (202) 223–8100
Website
http://www.indepsec.org

National leadership forum to encourage philanthropy, volunteering, not-for-profit initiatives and citizen action. Publications include the annual *The Nonprofit Almanac*

Institute for Charitable Giving 500 N. Michigan Avenue Chicago, IL 60611 Telephone (800) 234–7777 Website http://www.institutecharitable giv.com	Seminars on major gifts solicitation, planned giving and capital campaigns
International Society for Third-Sector Research The Johns Hopkins University Institute for Policy Studies Wyman Park Building, 5th Floor 3400 N. Charles Street Baltimore, MD 21218 Telephone (410) 516–4678 Website http://www.jhu.edu/~istr	Promotes research and education in the fields of philanthropy, civil society and the non-profit sector via publications and a biennial international conference.
Jospeh and Matthew Payton Philanthropic Studies Library Indiana University Purdue University University Library 755 West Michigan Street Indianapolis, IN 46202–5195 Telephone (317) 278–2311 E-mail jhuettne@indyvax.iupui.edu	Books, periodicals, annual reports, microform holdings, research papers. Topics include social movements, ethical and moral issues, non-profit organization management, religion and fund raising. Many out-of-print sources.
National Catholic Development Conference 86 Front Street Hempstead, NY 11550 Telephone (888) 879-6232	National association of Catholic organizations. Fund- raising training emphasizes ethics and accountability. Annual conference, annual leadership institute, regional workshops, newsletter published 10 times per year.

National Center
for Nonprofit Boards
2000 LStreet NW, Suite 510
Washington, DC 20036–4907
Telephone (202)452–6262
Fax (202) 452–6299
Website http://www.ncnb.org

Workshops, training programs,
publications

National Charitites
Information Bureau
19 Union Square West
New York, NY 10003–3395
Telephone (212) 929–6300
Website http://www.give.org

Compiles information on
charitable organizations to
enable contributors to make
sound giving decisions.
Publishes reports on individual
charities and *Wise Giving Guide.*

National Committee on
Planned Giving
233 McCrea Street, Suite 400
Indianopolis, IN 46225
Telephone (317) 269–6274
E-mail byeager@iupui.edu

Publications include a monthly
newsletter, guidelines on
starting a planned giving
program, and a kit on a
community-based program for
raising awareness about
planned giving.

National Committee
for Responsive Philanthropy
2001 S. Street, NW, Suite 620
Washington, DC 20009
Telephone (202) 387–9177
E-mail ncrp@aol.com

Publications include *The New
Age of Nonprofit Accountability*

National Council of Churches
of Christ in the USA
475 Riverside Drive, Suite 860
New York, NY 10115–0050
Telephone (212) 870–2383

Publishes *The Yearbook of
American and Canadian Churches*

National Federation
of Nonprofits
815 Fifteenth Street NW,
Suite 822
Washington, DC 20005–2201
Telephone (202) 628–4380
E-mail fnfndc@aol.com

Publications include *Eligibility
for nonprofit Postage Rates*

National Planned
Giving Institute
College of William and Mary
Gabrial Galt Building
P. O. Box 8795
Williamsburg, VA 23187-8795
Telephone (800) 249–0179
Fax (757) 221–1478
E-mail npgi@facstaff.wm.edu
Website
http://www.wm.edu/npgi

Training programs for major
current and deferred giving
offered in Williamsburg,
Memphis and Colorado
Springs

National Society of
Fund Raising Executives
1101 King Street, Suite 700
Alexandria, VA 22314–2967
Telephone (800) 666-3863
Fax (703) 684–0540
E-mail nsfre@nsfre.org
Website http://www.nsfre.org

Membership organization with
local chapters throughout the
world provides conferences,
courses in fund raising,
leadership and management
institutes, research library,
books and materials,
certification

Nonprofit Sector Research
Fund
1333 New Hampshire Avenue
NW
Suite 1070
Washington, DC 20036
Telephone (202) 736–5800

Publications include
Nonprofit Research News

Support Centers for
Nonprofit Management
706 Mission Street, Fifth Floor
San Francisco, CA
94103–3113
Telephone (415) 541–9000
Fax (415) 541–7708
Website
http://www.supportcenter.org/
sf/

Consulting, workshops,
publications, management
programs.

Appendix V

A Guide to Selecting Fund-Raising Counsel

Used by permission of the
American Association of Fund-Raising Counsel

When to Consider Counsel

- **Special Projects.** When an organization is building an endowment, financing a capital expansion or improvement, or increasing the scope of its programs, it may require intensive fund-raising efforts.

- **Increase or Establish Fund-Raising Revenue.** Some organizations that rely heavily or exclusively on other sources of funding, such as government contracts or fees for services, may decide to augment the role of voluntary contributions in their revenue mix.

- **Evaluate or Refresh Current Fund-Raising Programs.** An organization that has a well-established fund-raising program may wish to examine the program with a view toward updating or fine-tuning it.

- **Transition from Short-Term to Long-Term Planning.** Organizations that were established to address a crisis or a short-term need may discover after a period that the goal is still a long way from realization and requires a long-term direction. (Finding a cure for a disease is an example of such a goal.) Others, once uncertain about their long-term viability, begin to envision the organization as potentially having a long future. In these cases, more sophisticated and long-range fund-raising strategies will be required.

- **Strategic Development Planning.** Sometimes an organization perceives the need for improved fund-raising planning, when the latent, but more compelling, need is in some other place in the organization's structure. For example, needs that are manifestly connected to fund raising in fact may be the product of a need for board development or endowment building or for better marketing and communications strategies.

Services of Counsel
- Annual campaigns
- Capital campaigns (resident or off-site)
- Endowment development
- Feasibility studies
- Benefits
- Mail services
- Major gift development
- Telemarketing/communications
- Foundation and corporate giving support and strategies
- Grant writing
- Prospect research
- Pre-campaign positioning

- Planned giving program support and strategies
- Board development
- Volunteer recruitment
- Leadership, staff, volunteer or board training
- Interim staffing
- Serve as development office
- Start-up development office
- Student recruitment

Selecting Counsel
Step #1 - Identifying Prospective Consultants

Once the board and staff leadership have affirmed the desire to investigate fund-raising consultants or consulting firms, they can identify a pool of candidates via three main avenues:

- **Referrals.** Ask board members or colleagues.

- **Directories.** The AAFRC directory or others are excellent sources of information.

- **Advertisements.** Respond to advertisements in trade periodicals or the yellow pages.

Step #2 - Preliminary Screening

- **Basic Information.** Request basic information from each firm. Find out generally what kinds of services they provide to get an overview.

- **Detailed Information.** Narrow the field to three or four candidates and arrange a face-to-face briefing with each.

Step #3 - Request for Proposals

- **Proposal Content.** After the briefing, request proposals from each of the firms you meet with. Proposals should clearly state the costs, fees, services, and a preliminary schedule.

Step #4 - Check References

- **Calling References.** Always ask for references; always check them carefully. Ask the client if they would hire the firm again.

- **Successful and Unsuccessful Campaigns.** Ask for three references from satisfied clients and one reference from a client whose goal was not achieved or where the firm or the organization resigned from the contract. Firms should treat the request for a reference from a less-than-satisfied client as standard operating procedure.

Step #5 - Chemistry

There are many ways of knowing about a subject and of applying that knowledge when making a decision.

- **Impressions.** Your personal impression of key staff people will influence your decision.

- **Objectivity.** The search for a consultant should be as objective as possible, de-emphasizing where possible preferences about such factors as attire.

- **Being Realistic.** On the other hand, personal preferences are part of every professional relationship and every hiring decision. If you really do not relate well to someone when he or she is trying to impress you, chances are the relationship will not grow fonder.

- **Professional Judgment.** Instincts sometimes arise from wisdom. You should trust them but not allow them to overshadow the facts.

Step #6 - Notifying Candidates

- **Notify Everyone.** Notify all candidates of your decision. It is considered a courtesy to explain briefly the reasons for your choice to the consultants you did not select.

Step #7 - Contracts

The contract is very important and should be specific and detailed. This is the best time to uncover and iron out specific expectations or misunderstandings. Legal counsel should be consulted regarding specific appropriate terms and their wording in the document. The following matters, as well as others recommended by the organization's board or legal advisor, should be elucidated in detail in a contract or a letter serving as a contract:

- **Services.** What services will be provided? When and how often will you receive reports, and what will they contain?

- **Schedule.** Time period. If the period is expressed in days, how many hours is the day? If it is a planning or feasibility study, when will it start, and when will it be finished?

- **Fees.** What specific professional fees will be billed? What is the billing schedule? What additional expenses will be reimbursed by the client, up to what amount? (Fees should always be based upon services rendered. Never allow fees to be based upon the goal of the campaign. Contingency fund raising is prohibited by premier firms and eschewed by ethical consultants.)

- **Custody of Funds.** All funds raised for your organization should go directly to you. Do not permit counsel to maintain custody of funds.

- **Termination Clauses.** Under what conditions may the agreement be terminated by either party?

- **Personnel.** Which people from the firm will provide direct services, and what other professionals may be called upon to support them?

- **Fiscal Responsibility.** Who in the organization is responsible for contractual decisions, and who is responsible for rendering payment?

- **Location.** Where will services be rendered, on-site or off-site?

Step #8 - State Regulations

- **Compliance.** Most states require both charities and fund-raising professionals to register and follow certain procedures before commencing a campaign. Make sure both the organization and the fund raiser are in compliance.

- **Summary of State Laws.** A summary of the state laws, including the addresses and telephone numbers of state regulatory entities, is available from the AAFRC Trust for Philanthropy.

Areas of Potential Difficulty

- **Switching Consultants.** While changing consultants is a completely legal option and one appropriately exercised if you are truly dissatisfied, the firm that does your feasibility study or begins your campaign develops a knowledge of your organization and constituency that goes beyond the parameters of even the most thorough and detailed report. A great deal of accumulated wisdom is lost when bringing in a new firm midway through a process.

- **The Lowest Bid.** Each campaign should be designed specifically for your organization and should not be shaped with a cookie-cutter approach. Even responsible bids vary, and you have to use professional judgment and fact checking to know what you really want. Sometimes the lowest bid is the best one, but not necessarily.

- **Communication With Donors.** The relationship between a charity and its donors is precious and should continue long after counsel has left. Anything that comes between an organization and its constituency is detrimental to long-term viability and the organization's potential to fulfill its mission. Staff, board members, or volunteers should ask for donations, not counsel. Written communications as well as verbal ones should be developed with scrupulous oversight from the organization.

- **Interviewing too Many Firms.** After a point, the process of interviewing consultants becomes repetitive, frustrating, and too time-consuming for staff and volunteers. Three firms are plenty; more than four begins to be counterproductive.

Appendix VI

Sample Contracts of Consultants

These composite samples are for educational purposes only and are not intended to provide legal advice. Please consult with your attorney before entering into any legal agreement.

A. Three-Month Contract for A Specific Project

AN AGREEMENT

This Agreement entered into this 8th (Eighth) day of April, 1993 by and between Gateway Community Church (Client) and Fred A. Hampton and Associates (Consultant).

This Agreement shall be governed by the following provisions:

1.   The term of this Agreement shall begin on the 8th (Eighth) day of April 1993 and end on the 8th (Eighth) day of July, 1993.

2.   Consultant is an independent contractor, who, during the term of this Agreement, shall provide Client with the following services:

    a. Assist and advise in creating a written Annual Fund System to enable Client to secure recurring gift income from a variety of sources, including individuals, corporations, and organizations.

    b. Unlimited telephone consultations during regular business hours.

    c. Up to 18 (Eighteen) hours of face-to-face consultations at the base fee specified in Section 5 (Five) Paragraph a. below.

    d. Consultant's best opinions and recommendations based on his knowledge, experience and training. Implementation of Consultant's opinions and recommendations shall be in the sole discretion of Client. In no case shall Consultant make decisions for Client.

3.   Information obtained by Consultant in the performance of services shall be strictly confidential. Consultant shall not publish nor disclose this information to others nor authorize others to do so without prior written consent of Client. At the end of this Agreement, Consultant shall return to Client all Client-owned materials which may have been in the temporary possession of Consultant for purposes of providing Consultant's Services.

4.   Client shall cooperate in all ways possible to assist Consultant in the successful performance of Consultant's Services, including, but not limited to, sharing information with Consultant regarding Client's donor and prospect records, correspondence, special events, methods for identifying, cultivating and soliciting donors and prospective donors, and fund-raising activities of all kinds.

5.   For Consultant's Services during the term of this Agreement, Client shall pay Consultant as follows:

    a. A base fee of $1,800 (One-Thousand Eight-Hundred Dollars) in equal parts of $600 (Six-

Hundred Dollars), each part billed to Client monthly beginning in May 1993.

b. $100 (One-Hundred Dollars) per hour or portion thereof in one-half-hour increments for face-to-face consultations which occur after the first 18 (Eighteen) hours of face-to-face consultations, billed to Client monthly, beginning in the month following the first occurrence.

c. Out-of-pocket expenses including but not limited to expenses for photocopies, facsimiles, long-distance telephone calls, automobile rental, public transportation, lodging, meals and automobile mileage, billed to Client monthly beginning in May 1993. Automobile mileage shall be billed at 40-cents (Forty-Cents) per mile.

6. This Agreement may be amended only in writing.

Signed this 8th (Eighth) day of April 1993.

Marilyn Krause, Chairperson
Board of Trustees
Gateway Community Church

Fred A. Hampton, President
Fred A. Hampton and
Associates Consultant

B. Letter Contract for A Capital Campaign

Dear Ms. Krause:

Thanks for your confidence in us to assist Gateway Community Church with your building plans. We were pleased to conduct the feasibility study which confirmed that now is the time to initiate a campaign for a new sanctuary. Many church members are ready to enthusiastically support this important project and to enlist the support of others.

To assist your team in preparing for and completing a successful campaign, we propose meeting with you and other leaders once monthly during the next 15 months, beginning in May 1995 and ending in July 1996. Either party may cancel on 90 days written notice.

We would advise all aspects of the campaign, including:

1. Budget, program planning, and organizing
2. Strategies to secure leadership gifts and other major gifts
3. Planned giving policies and procedures
4. Committee assignments and job descriptions
5. Training for board members and other volunteers
6. Prospect identification, research, cultivation, and solicitation
7. Donor recognition
8. Writing and designing the case statement and other publications
9. News releases and publicity
10. Victory celebration event

Our fee is $1,500 per day and expenses. Expenses include, but are not limited to, travel, meals, lodging, printing, postage, and shipping. You may call us anytime during business hours for free unlimited telephone consultations.

If this proposal is satisfactory, please sign below, return the original to us, and keep a copy for your records.

We look forward to working with you to achieve your goals.

Sincerely,

Fred A. Hampton, President

Accepted for Gateway Community Church by:

_____

Marilyn Krause, Chairperson
Board of Trustees

Date _____

Appendix VII

World Wide Web Resources

The Alta Vista search engine lists more than 500,000 sites indexed to the words *fund raising* and *fundraising*, more than 525,000 to the word *nonprofit*, more than 150,000 to the word *stewardship*, and more than 110,000 to the word *philanthropy*. Listed here are sites the authors have found helpful. The information at the sites is free. Some sites offer services and products for sale. Many have links to other sites with related information.

To Learn More About	Visit These Sites
Assets, liabilities, revenues and expenditures of nonprofits; tips for donors; non-profit news	www.guidestar.org Provider, GuideStar/ Philanthropic Research, Inc.
Board member newsletter delivered free by e-mail each month	http://www.support center.org/sf/publications board_cafe/boardcafe.html Provider, Support Center for Nonprofit Management

Books on fund raising and stewardship, from publishers	htttp://www.ecpa.org Provider, Evangelical Christian Publishers Association http://www.wiley.com/nonprofit Provider, John Wiley & Sons http://www.josseybass.com/ Provider, Jossey-Bass Publishers http://www.bonus-books.com/precept/subject/funds/index.html Provider, Precept Press
Books on fund raising and stewardship, from book sellers	http://amazon.com Provider, Amazon Books http://barnesandnoble.com Provider, Barnes and Noble
Building stronger non-profit boards	http://www.ncnb.org/ Provider, National Center for Nonprofit Boards
Canadian non-profit news, jobs, information, and resources	http://www.charityvillage.com/cvhome.html Provider, Charity Village/Hilborn Interactive, Inc.
Certificate in Nonprofit Leadership and Management via satellite download to your community	http://www.pbs.org/learnals/nonprofit/ Provider, Public Broadcasting Service Adult Learning Service
Creating fund-raising programs and evaluating non-profit programs	http://www.inetwork.org Provider, Innovation Network, Inc.
Donor research and prospect identification	http://philanthropy.com Provider, The Chronicle of Philanthropy
Ethics training	http://www.josephsoninstitute.org/ Provider, The Josephson Institute

Evaluating non-profit programs	http://www.unitedway.org/outcomes Provider, United Way of America
Fund raising and non-profit management	http://www.fic-ftw.org/ Provider, Funding InformationCenter/ Foundation Center http://www.supportcenter.org/sca/ Provider, Support Centers of America
Fund-raising techniques and chapters of fund-raising executives	http://www.nsfre.org/ Provider, National Society of Fund Raising Executives
Global directory of non-profit organizations	http://www.idealist.org Provider, Action Without Borders
Grant writing and directories	http://www.fdncenter.org Provider, The Foundation Center http://www.tgci.com Provider, The Grantsmanship Center http://www.thomson.com/gale/taftcat.html Provider, The Taft Group
Internet sites for and about nonprofits	http://www.clark.net/pub/pwalker/ Provider, Philip A. Walker
Legal issues and research	http://www.not-for-profit.org Provider, Nonprofits, Inc.
Non-profit news and resources	http://www.gilbert.org Provider, The Gilbert Center

Philanthropy, volunteering, non-profit initiatives and citizen action.	http://www.indepsec.org/ Provider, Independent Sector
Planned giving	http://www.ncpg.org Provider, National Committee on Planned Giving http://www.libertel. montreal.gc.ca/info/acpdp/ gpicplus/english/ resources.html Provider, Canadian Association of Gift Planners
Products and services offered by companies that specialize in serving nonprofits	http://philanthropy.com Provider, *The Chronicle of Philanthropy* http:/danenet.wicip.org/snpo Provider, the Society for Nonprofit Organizations
Resources and news on fund raising, foundations, corporate giving, technology and research; free newsletter delivered by e-mail	http://www.philanthropy-journal.org/ Provider, Philanthropy Journal Online
Social justice, human rights and environmental organizations	http://www.igc.org/ Provider, Institute for Global Communications
Software to help nonprofits with fund raising, marketing, supervising volunteers, and other areas	http://www.shu.edu/ ~kleintwi/tnlpsi/tnopsi.html Provider, Center for Public Service, Seton Hall University
Technology to improve nonprofits	http:/www.uwnyc.org/ tech.htm Provider, United Way of New York http://www.igc.org/trc Provider, Technology Resource Consortium/ Nonprofit Management Association

Using e-mail and the World-Wide Web; free newsletter delivered by e-mail	Send an e-mail message to majordomo@listbox.com. Type "subscribe netresults" in the message box. Provider, Lipman Hearne
Volunteer opportunities and using the Internet	http://www.impactonline.org Provider, Impact Online
Which organizations qualify to receive tax-deductible charitable contributions, information on charitable contributions	http://www.irs.ustreas.gov/ Click on *Tax Info For You* then click on *Exempt Organizations.* Provider, Internal Revenue Service
Wise giving practices and issues of concern to donors and volunteers	http://www.nonprofits.org/ Provider, Internet Nonprofit Center http://www.bbb.org Provider, Philanthropic Advisory Service of the Better Business Bureau

Appendix VIII

Sample Foundation Bylaws

*Used by permission of Council of Churches of the
Ozarks Foundation, Inc. Check with your attorney for the
applicable laws in your state.*

BYLAWS OF
COUNCIL OF CHURCHES OF THE
OZARKS FOUNDATION, INC.

ARTICLE I
PURPOSE

Section 1. Primary Purpose. The Council of Churches of the Ozarks Foundation, Inc. (the "Foundation") is a corporation organized exclusively for charitable purposes as set forth in its Articles of Incorporation and more specifically set forth herein. The primary purpose of the Foundation is to support the Council of Churches of the Ozarks, including any successor thereof (the "Council"). The Foundation is intended to expand and enrich the mission of the

Council. The Foundation is created as an expression of the belief that people of faith are called to be faithful managers of all the gifts of God. The objectives of the Foundation are to provide members and friends of the Council with a means to make gifts which will continue to support the Council's mission in perpetuity; to provide the Council with additional financial strength to carry out its ministries; to counsel members and friends of the Council seeking advice on making gifts to the Council or Foundation, which counsel may include referral to qualified legal and financial advisors; to educate members and friends of the Council about the importance of personal financial planning and the opportunities for charitable giving; and to invest and manage assets in a manner consistent with the Foundation's mission and the wishes of donors.

Section 2. Duties. In carrying out its purposes, the Foundation will

(a) Undertake educational activities, including guidance of personal stewardship, classes and seminars on financial planning, encouragement of gifts and bequests, and placement of notices and reminders of planned giving in Council publications and mailings;

(b) Assume responsibility for the receipt, safekeeping, investment, management, conveyance and distribution of the Foundation's assets;

(c) Present to the Council, by the first of May of each year, a report on the Foundation's status and activities for the preceding year, the report to include an audit of the Foundation's accounts;

(d) Distribute to the Council, or to projects designated by the Council, annually by June 1 the greater of (1) the income of the Foundation for the preceding year, net of expenses of administering the Foundation and its assets and not including the income of the Reserve Fund, or (2) five percent of the value of the Foundation's investment assets at the end of the preceding year. In addition, the Foundation may, in the discretion of the directors, distribute annually as much as two-thirds of the increase in the value of the

Foundation's investment assets (other than assets in the Reserve Fund) during the preceding year. The value of the investment assets and the amount of growth in value shall be determined by the directors in a reasonable manner; in the case of assets which would be difficult or expensive to value, the directors may use either the book value or a reasonable estimate of the market value of such assets;

(e) Maintain a Book of Gifts recording gifts received and relevant data concerning such gifts, except where the donor of the gift wishes to be anonymous, including gifts made through wills and trust agreements, deferred gifts, outright gifts and memorial gifts; and the Board may establish policies for proper acknowledgment of and credit for gifts other than outright gifts;

(f) Publish at least annually a list of memorials and donors and other relevant material, and distribute the publication to the Council and others the directors may designate;

(g) Maintain financial records, audited at least every two years, and make the financial records available for review; and

(h) Protect and safeguard the funds of the Foundation for the Foundation's purposes and consistent with the limitations of the Articles of Incorporation and these Bylaws.

ARTICLE II
CONTRIBUTIONS

Section 1. Acceptance of Contributions. The Board of Directors (the "Board") shall determine whether or not to accept any contribution to the Foundation, and no contribution shall be deemed accepted without the approval of the Board. The Board may accept gifts in trust and administer trusts thus established. The Board shall not accept, without the approval of the Council, a contribution designated for projects or purposes other than those engaged in by the Council.

Section 2. Named Funds. A gift of five thousand dollars or more in value may be accepted as a separate fund to be known by the name of the donor or a person identified by the donor.

Section 3. Absence of Directions. In the absence of contrary directions by a contributor to the Foundation, the following shall apply:

(a) Property contributed to the Foundation may be retained or sold and reinvested as the Board directs;

(b) Investment assets of the Foundation will be considered as endowed funds, to be held in perpetuity unless allocated to the Reserve Fund or distributed in accordance with the annual distribution requirements set forth in these Bylaws.

ARTICLE III
DIRECTORS

Section 1. Powers. All corporate powers shall be exercised by or under the authority of the Board, and the business and affairs of the Foundation shall be controlled by the Board, subject to limitations of the Articles of Incorporation, these Bylaws, the Missouri Nonprofit Corporations Act, and the duties prescribed herein. In addition to general corporate powers, the Board shall have the power:

(a) To alter, amend or repeal the Articles of Incorporation and these Bylaws by the approval of not less than eight percent of the directors;

(b) To select and remove all officers, agents and employees of the Foundation, prescribe their powers and duties, and fix their compensation;

(c) To employ investment managers and custodians, which shall have any appropriate license, registration and surety, and discharge the same as the Board deems advisable in the management of the Foundation's investments;

(d) To appoint committees and to delegate to such committees any of the powers an authority of the Board in the management of the business and affairs of the

Foundation, except the powers to amend the Articles of Incorporation or to adopt, amend or repeal bylaws; any such committee shall be composed of one or more directors of the Foundation, and may include directors or officers of the Council. At such time as the number of directors of the Foundation exceeds seven, the Board shall appoint an executive committee of five directors to conduct the ordinary business of the Foundation; and

(e) To authorize any officer or officers or agent or agents of the Foundation to enter into any contract or execute any instrument in the name of and on behalf of the Foundation, either in general or in specific instances.

Section 2. Number. The initial Board shall consist of the persons designated by the incorporator as provided in the Articles of Incorporation. Thereafter, the number of directors shall not be less than seven nor more than fifteen persons. A person must be at least thirty-five years of age to be eligible to be a director. The President of the Council shall be a director of the Foundation, and when the number of the directors of the Foundation reaches ten, the Council shall have the right to add two of its directors to the Foundation's Board, in addition to the directors of the Foundation then serving. The Director of the Council shall be entitled to attend meetings of the Board but shall not have a vote.

Section 3. Term. Each director other than the director who is President of the Council shall hold office for a term of three years, except that the initial directors shall have terms of one, two or three years, as specified by the incorporator, in order to produce staggered terms. No person shall be a director for more than two consecutive three-year terms, and having served two consecutive three-year terms, a person shall not be elected to the Board within one year of the expiration of the most recent term. The Board shall elect directors to replace directors whose terms have expired and shall appoint a nominating committee, with directors of the Foundation being a majority of the members of such committee, to nominate persons to be elected to the Board.

A director may be removed at any time, with or without cause, by the vote of a majority of the other directors. In case of the death, resignation or removal of one or more of the directors of the Foundation, a majority of the remaining directors may fill the vacancy or vacancies at any time.

Section 4. Place of Meetings: Annual and Regular Meetings.

(a) All meetings of the board of the Foundation may be held within or without the State of Missouri as may be provided in the resolution or notice calling such meeting.

(b) The annual meeting of the directors for the purpose of electing officers, directors and transacting such other business as may come before the meeting shall be held on the first Wednesday of June of each year. No notice of such annual meeting of the directors need be given. If for any reason such annual meeting of the directors is not or cannot be held on that date, the officers may be elected at the first meeting of the directors thereafter called or held pursuant to these Bylaws. Quarterly meetings of the Board shall be held at such times as the Board may from time to time provide and without any notice other than the resolution or action providing for such meetings.

Section 5. Special Meetings. Special meetings of the Board may be called at any time upon the call of the President or at least twenty percent of the directors then in office. Written notice of all special meetings of the Board shall be given to each director which notice shall state the time, place and purpose of such meeting, and shall be mailed to each director at least five days before such meeting, addressed to the last known residence or place of business of each director.

Section 6. Waiver of Notice. Attendance of a director at any meeting, whether regular or special, constitutes a waiver of notice of such meeting except where a director attends a meeting for the express purpose of objecting to the transaction of any business because the meeting is not lawfully called or convened. If any meeting of the directors be irregular for want of notice, provided a quorum was present at such meeting, the proceedings of such meeting may be ratified and approved and rendered likewise valid, and the irregularity or defect therein waived, by a writing signed by all persons having the right to vote at such meeting. Whenever any notice is required to be given to any director under any provisions of these Bylaws, a waiver in writing, signed by the persons entitled to notice, shall be deemed equivalent to notice.

Section 7. Quorum. A majority of the Board shall constitute a quorum for the transaction of business, and the act of the majority of the directors present at a meeting at which a quorum is present shall be valid as a corporate act, except as may be otherwise specifically required by law, the Articles of Incorporation, or these Bylaws. If less than a quorum be present at any meeting, those present may adjourn from time to time and fix dates for subsequent meetings until a quorum shall be present.

Section 8. Action Without Meeting: Meetings by Telephone.

(a) The Board may take or approve action or adopt resolutions without a meeting with the full force and effect as if such action was taken or approved or such resolutions adopted by motion duly made and unanimously carried at a meeting duly called, noticed and held, if all the voting members of the Board execute a written instrument setting forth the action to be taken or approved or the resolution adopted. The action so taken or approved, or the resolution so adopted shall be deemed taken, approved, or adopted at a meeting held on the date set forth therein and if such unanimous consent be obtained, the officers are authorized to certify that such acts or resolutions were taken, approved, or adopted at a meeting duly noticed, called, and held in any instrument filed with third parties thereafter.

(b) Directors may participate in a meeting of the Board (or committee) by means of conference telephone or similar communications equipment by which all directors participating simultaneously hear each other during the meeting. All persons participating in a meeting by means of such equipment shall be deemed present in person at the meeting.

Section 9. Salaries. Directors as such shall not receive any salary for their services; provided that nothing herein contained shall be construed to preclude any director from serving the Foundation in any other capacity (e.g., as officer, agent, employee, or otherwise) and receiving compensation therefor.

ARTICLE IV
OFFICERS

Section 1. Officers. The officers of the Foundation shall be a Chairman of the Board, a President, a Secretary, and a Treasurer, and such other additional officers as the Board may from time to time elect. Any two or more offices may be held by the same individual.

Section 2. Election and Term. The initial officers shall be elected at the first meeting of the Board and thereafter shall be elected at the annual meeting of the Board. The officers shall hold office at the pleasure of the Board from the dates of their respective elections and may be removed at any time with or without cause by the Board. Absent prior removal by the directors, the officers shall continue in office from the date of their respective elections until their successors are duly elected and qualified.

Section 3. The Chairman of the Board. The Chairman of the Board shall preside at all meetings of the Board at which he or she shall be present. The chairman shall perform all the duties as are incident to the office or as are required by law, the Bylaws, or the Board.

Section 4. The President. The President shall be the chief executive of the Foundation and shall have general supervision of the business and finances of the Foundation, shall see that all orders and resolutions of the Board are carried into effect, and shall, in the absence of the Chairman of the Board, preside at all meetings of the Board subject, however, to the right of all directors to delegate any specific powers to any other officer or officers of the Foundation.

The President shall perform all duties incident to the office of the President and as are given to the President by the Bylaws or as may from time to time be assigned to the President by the Board. The President shall act as the duly authorized representative of the Board and of the Foundation in all matters in which the Board has not formally designated some other person to so act.

Section 5. The Secretary. The Secretary shall serve as secretary of the meetings of the Board, shall give or cause to be given all required notice of meetings of the directors, record all proceedings of the meetings of the directors in books to be kept for that purpose, perform all duties incident to the office that are properly required by him or her by the Board or the President. It shall be the duty of the Secretary to obtain and record the address of each director and officer. The Board at any meeting may designate any of their number or any assistant secretary to act as temporary secretary in the absence of the Secretary.

Section 6. The Treasurer. The Treasurer shall have the custody of the Foundation's funds and securities, shall keep full and accurate accounts of money and disbursements in books belonging to the Foundation, and shall deposit all monies and other valuable effects in the name and to the credit of the Foundation in such depositories as shall be designated by the Board. The Treasurer shall cause to be filed with such governmental agencies all reports and returns relating to the Foundation's operating results or financial condition as shall be required. The Treasurer shall disburse such funds of the Foundation as may be ordered by the Board and render to the Board, in such detail and for such periods as the Board shall request, a report on all of his or her transactions as treasurer and furnish to the Board a report on the operating results and financial condition of the Foundation., And further, the Treasurer shall

(a) Institute the calendar year as the fiscal year of the Foundation, until otherwise directed by the Board;

(b) Establish three separate funds for contributions to the Foundation: a Designated Fund for contributions which were designated by donors, and accepted by the Board, for a specific purpose; an Undesignated Fund for contributions which were not designated for a specific purpose; and a Reserve Fund for assets the Board desires to be set aside for future expenditure or distribution for a specific purpose; and

(c) Direct investment advisors to divest any investments in companies whose purposes or practices are contrary to Christian moral or ethical principles, as determined by the Board.

Section 7. Other Officers. The Board may elect such subordinate officers as it may deem desirable. Each such officer shall have such authority and perform such duties as the Board may prescribe. The Board may from time to time authorize any officer to appoint such officers and to prescribe the powers and duties thereof.

ARTICLE V
INDEMNIFICATION OF OFFICERS
AND DIRECTORS

Section 1. Liability. A director or officer of the Foundation acting in good faith and in a manner reasonably believed by the director or officer to be in the best interests of the Foundation shall not be liable to the Foundation, and shall be indemnified by the Foundation against liability to third parties, for actions taken in such capacity.

Section 2. Insurance. The Foundation may purchase insurance on behalf of any officer or director of the Foundation against any liability asserted against or incurred by him or her in such capacity.

ARTICLE VI
DISSOLUTION

The Foundation is intended to continue as long as the Council exists. If the Council ceases to exist, the Foundation shall be terminated and its assets distributed as provided in the Articles of Incorporation. The Foundation shall not be dissolved while the Council exists except with the approval of not less that eighty percent of the directors.

Appendix IX

For Further Reading

Twenty-five years ago the available literature on fund raising would just about have filled two type-written pages, even less on church fund raising. In recent years there has been an explosion of publications. Our list is intended to be representative, not exhaustive. The books were selected to get you started in your search for what works.

Other listings can be obtained from your local library or bookstore, the National Society of Fund Raising Executives (NSFRE), and *The Chronicle of Philanthropy*. NSFRE's address is 1101 King Street, Suite 700, Alexandria, VA 22314-2967, telephone 800-666-3863, e-mail sales@nsfre.org. Their Web site is http://www.nsfre.org. *The Chronicle of Philanthropy*, a bi-weekly newspaper, publishes an annual supplement, *The Non-Profit Handbook*. Order from *The Chronicle of Philanthropy*, P.O. Box 1989, Marion, Ohio 43305-1989, telephone 800-728-2819, e-mail subscriptions@philanthropy.com. Their Web site is http://philanthropy.com.

We have included books on related topics, including stewardship sermons, boards, volunteers, budgeting, special events, and the offertory.

Albert Anderson, *Ethics for Fundraisers*, Indiana University Press, Bloomington, 1996.

Kermit L. Braswsell, *Step by Step: A Financial Campaign for Your Church*, Abingdon Press, Nashville, 1995.

Kenneth H. Blanchard and Norman Vincent Peale, *The Power of Ethical Management: Why the Ethical Way is the Profitable Way, in Your Life & in Your Business*, William Morrow & Company, New York, 1988.

Ken Burnett, *Relationship Fundraising*, Precept Press, Chicago, 1995.

Kennon L. Callahan, *Giving and Stewardship in an Effective Church: A Guide for Every Member*, Jossey-Boss, San Francisco, 1992.

Mim Carlson, *Winning Grants Step by Step: Support Centers of America's Complete Workbook for Planning, Developing, and Writing Successful Proposals*, Jossey-Bass, San Francisco, 1995.

Barbara Kushner Ciconte and Jeanne G. Jacob, *Fund Raising Basics: A Complete Guide*, Aspen Publishers, Gaithersburg, Maryland, 1997.

Charles Cloughen, *One Minute Stewardship Sermons*, Morehouse Publishing, Harrisburg, Pennsylvania, 1997.

Stephen R. Covey, A. Roger Merrill, Rebecca R. Merrill, *First Things First: To Live, to Love, to Learn, to Leave a Legacy*, reprint edition, Simon and Schuster, New York, 1996.

James A. Donovan *Take the Fear Out of Asking for Major Gifts*, Donovan Management, Winter Springs, Florida, 1994.

Kent E. Dove, *Conducting A Successful Capital Campaign: A Comprehensive Fundraising Guide for Nonprofit Organizations*, Jossey-Bass, San Francisco, 1988.

Murray Dropkin and Bill LaTouche, *The Budget Building Book: A Step-by-Step Guide for Nonprofit Managers and Boards*, Jossey-Bass, San Francisco, 1998.

Chuck Elliot, *Aspen's Guide to 60 Successful Special Events*, Aspen Publishers, Gaithersburg, Maryland, 1995.

Arthur C. Frantzreb, *Not on This Board You Don't: Making Your Trustees More Effective*, Bonus Books, Chicago, 1996.

Micki Gordon, *The Fundraising Manual: A Step by Step Guide to Creating the Perfect Event*, The FIG Press, Gaithersburg, Maryland, 1997.

Ashley Hale, *The Lost Art of Church Fund Raising*, Precept Press, Chicago, 1993.

Robert F. Hartsook, *Closing That Gift!*, ASR Philanthropic Publishing, Wichita, 1998.

David L. Heetland, *Fundamentals of Fund Raising*, Discipleship Resources, Nashville, 1989.

Dean R. Hoge, Charles Zech, Patrick McNamara, Michael J. Donahue, *Money Matters: Personal Giving in American Churches*, Westminster John Knox Press, Louisville, 1996.

Fisher Howe, *The Board Member's Guide to Fund Raising: What Every Trustee Needs to Know About Raising Money*, Jossey-Bass, San Francisco, 1991.

Douglas M. Lawson, *Give to Live: A Program of Joyful Giving for the Local Church*, Abingdon Press, Nashville, 1995. Includes leader's manual; two video tapes; one audio tape; Lawson's book, *Give to Live: How Giving Can Change Your Life*; and sample materials.

Stan L. Lequire, Editor, *The Best Preaching on Earth: Sermons on Caring for Creation*, Judson Press, Valley Forge, 1996.

Paul R. Lindholm, *First Fruits: Stewardship Thoughts and Stories from Around the World*, Hope Publishing House, Pasadena, California, 1993.

Mike Martin, *Virtuous Giving: Philanthropy, Voluntary Service and Caring*, Indiana University Press, Bloomington, 1993.

Steve McCurley and Rick Lynch, *Volunteer Management: Mobilizing all the Resources of the Community*, Heritage Arts Publishing, Downers Grove, Illinois, 1996.

Ray Miles, *Offering Meditations*, Chalice Press, St. Louis, 1998.

Lynda S. Moerschbaecher, *Start at Square One*, Bonus Books, Chicago, 1998.

Dan Moseley, Editor, *Joyful Giving: Sermons on Stewardship*, Abingdon Press, Nashville, 1997.

Judith E. Nichols, *Pinpointing Affluence: Increasing Your Share of Major Donor Dollars*, Precept Press, Chicago, 1994.

John L. Ronsvalle and Sylvia Ronsvalle, *Behind the Stained Glass Windows: Money Dynamics in the Church*, Baker Books, Ada, Michigan, 1996.

Henry A. Rosso, *Rosso on Fund Raising: Lessons from a Masters Lifetime Experience*, Jossey-Bass, San Francisco, 1996.

Larry C. Spears, Editor, *Insights on Leadership: Service, Stewardship, Spirit, and Servant-Leadership*, John Wiley & Sons, New York, 1997.

William T. Sturtevant, *The Artful Journey: Cultivating and Soliciting the Major Gift*, Bonus Books, Chicago, 1997.

Rick Warren, *The Purpose-Driven Church*, Zondervan, Grand Rapids, 1995.

William D. Watley, *Bring the Full Tithe: Sermons on the Grace of Giving*, Judson Press, Valley Forge, 1995.

Michael Webb, *Beyond Tithes and Offerings: A Closer Look at Traditional Giving and Its Impact on Christian Responsibility*, On Time Publishing, Tacoma, Washington, 1998.

Robert Wuthnow and Virginia A. Hodgkinson, *Faith and Philanthropy in America: Exploring the Role of Religion in America's Voluntary Sector*, Jossey-Bass, San Francisco, 1990.

Appendix X

Directories, Periodicals, and Subscription Services

Our list is intended to be representative, not exhaustive. Two of the best known publishers of directories are The Foundation Center and The Taft Group. They publish a wide variety of resources on corporate and foundation grantmakers, writing successful grant proposals, and guides to religious funding sources. To receive their catalogs, contact them at:

The Foundation Center
79 Fifth Avenue
New York, NY 10003-3076
Telephone 1-800-424-9836
Fax Ordering 212-807-3677
Web Site http://www.fdncenter.org

The Taft Group
P.O. Box 33477
Detroit, MI 48232-5477

Telephone 1-800-414-8238
Fax Ordering 1-800-414-5043
Internet Orders: galeord@gale.com
Web Site http://www.taftgroup.com

Board Leadership. Bi-monthly newsletter published by Jossey-Bass Publishers, 350 Sansome Street, San Francisco, CA 94104-9825. Telephone 800-956-7739. Fax 800-605-2665. Web site http://www.jossey-bass.com/.

Charitable Giving Tax Service. Kathryne Sperlak, Editor. Extensive library of materials in three-ring notebooks, updated bi-monthly. Published by R&R Newkirk, 8695 S. Archer, Suite 10, Willow Springs, IL 60480. Toll-free 800-342-2375. Fax 708-839-9207.

Clergy Finance Newsletter. Published bi-monthly by Clergy Financial Services, P.O. Box 6007, Grand Rapids, MI 49516. Telephone and Fax, 616-956-0087.

Contributions. Bi-monthly magazine published by Cambridge Fund Raising Associates, P.O. Box 338, Medfield, MA 02052. Telephone 508-359-0019. Fax 508-359-8084. E-mail contrib@ziplink.net.

Development Director's Letter. Monthly newsletter published by CD Publications, 8204 Fenton Street, Silver Spring, MD 20910. Telephone 800-666-6380.

Fund Raising Management. Monthly magazine published by Hoke Communications, 224 7th Street, Garden City, NY 11530. Telephone 516-746-6700. Toll-free 800-229-6700. Fax 516-294-8141. E-mail 71410.2423@compuserve.com.

Give & Take. Monthly newsletter published by Robert F. Sharpe and Company, 5050 Poplar Avenue, Suite 700, Memphis TN 38157. Telephone 901-680-5300. E-mail info@rfsco.com. Web site http://www.rfsco.com.

Money Matters. Monthly newsletter published by Christian Financial Concepts, 601 Broad Street SE, Gainesville, GA 30501. Telephone 800-722-1976.

The Nonprofit Board Report. Monthly newsletter published by The Nonprofit Board Report, 370 Technology Drive, Malvern, PA 19355. Telephone 800-220-8600.

Nonprofit Management and Leadership. Quarterly journal published by Jossey-Bass, Inc., 10900 Euclid Avenue, Cleveland, OH 44106-7164. Telephone 216-368-2315. Fax 216-368-8592. E-mail lks4@p.o.cwru.edu.

NonProfit Times. Monthly newspaper published by NPT Publishing Group, Inc., 240 Cedar Knolls Road, Suite 318, Cedar Knolls NJ 07927. Telephone 973-734-1700. E-mail circmngr@nptimes.com. Web site www.nptimes.com

The Philanthropic Dollar. Monthly newsletter publisher by Philanthropic Service for Institutions of the Seventh-day Adventist Church, 12501 Old Columbia Pike, Silver Spring, MD 20904-6600. Telephone 301680-6131. Fax 301-680-6137. Website http://northamerica.adventist.org/psi

Nonprofit World. Magazine published six times per year by the Society for Nonprofit Organizations, 6314 Odana Road, Suite One, Madison, WI 53719. Telephone 800-424-7367. Fax 608-274-9978. Email snpo@danenet.wicip.org Website http://danenet.wicip.org/snpo

Successful Fund Raising. Monthly newsletter published by Stevenson Consultants, Inc., P.O. Box 4528, Sioux City, Iowa 51104-9903. Telephone 712-239-3010. Fax 712-239-2166.

About the Authors

The Rev. Dr. Dorsey E. Levell is executive director of the Council of Churches of the Ozarks Foundation, Inc., Springfield, Missouri. He was named to the position in 1998 when he retired after thirty-one years as the founding executive director of the Council of Churches of the Ozarks. The Council operates fifteen human services programs, including a child care facility, a food bank, a rehabilitation treatment center, and a clothing distribution center. The services have 120 paid staff, more than 1,000 volunteers and an annual budget of $12 million dollars.

Dr. Levell was named Humanitarian of the Year in 1995 by the Community Foundation of the Ozarks and Springfieldian of the Year in 1990 by the Springfield Area Chamber of Commerce. He is a retired U.S. Army chaplain and colonel, an ordained minister of the United Methodist Church, and a former pastor. He is a charter member of the Springfield National Speakers Guild and a member of the National Society of Fund Raising Executives. He has spoken to many professional fund-raising groups and presented numerous workshops to churches and other nonprofits.

He took his bachelor's degree from Central Missouri State College and his master's degree from United Theological Seminary. He has honorary doctorates from the Forest Institute of Psychology and Drury College.

Wayne E. Groner, CFRE, is executive director of the Labette Community College Foundation and Alumni Association, Parsons, Kansas. He has been a fund-raising officer at private and public colleges since 1977, including nine years as a vice-president for development. Before getting into fund raising he lived in Springfield, Missouri, where he was a radio and television news reporter, owned a magazine publishing company, and twice was elected state representative to the Missouri General Assembly.

He earned the designation Certified Fund Raising Executive (CFRE) from the National Society of Fund Raising Executives (NSFRE). He organized chapters of NSFRE in Sioux City, Iowa, and Joplin, Missouri. He has been a workshop instructor for NSFRE, the Council for Advancement and Support of Education, and the Council for Resource Development. He has created and implemented marketing programs for annual giving, major gifts, planned gifts, and capital campaigns. He has designed, edited, and written alumni magazines, brochures, and direct mail pieces for fund raising.

He is an ordained minister of the Reorganized Church of Jesus Christ of Latter Day Saints, literacy tutor, hospice chaplain, and former pastor.

Let Us Hear From You

Your success is our success. After you have implemented the principles and practices of successful fund raising from our book, please let us know your results. Write to us at 3130 South Oak Street, Springfield, Missouri 65804.

If you would like information on scheduling us to speak or on conducting a workshop in your area, please write to the same address.